THE PERSONAL JOURNAL OF SOLOMON:
The Secrets of Kohelet

A commentary of Ecclesiastes for the common reader

By

Dr. Darryl DelHousaye
Dr. Bobby Brewer

PRESS

The Personal Journal of Solomon:
The Secrets of Kohelet
by Dr. Darryl DelHousaye and Dr. Bobby Brewer

Printed in the United States of America

ISBN 978-1-60647-114-2

www.xulonpress.com

Other Books by the Authors:

Darryl DelHousaye:
Servant Leadership: The Seven Distinctive Characteristics of a Servant Leader
Ask Pastor Darryl:121 Answers to Frequently Asked Bible Questions
Today for Eternity (devotional)
Study notes for the Nelson Study Bible (Acts)

Bobby Brewer:
Postmodernism: What You Should Know & Do About It
UFOs: 7 Things You Should Know
Two other books, co-authored with Dr. DelHousaye

Dedicated to

—ᴍ—

John and Kent DelHousaye
two sons who have chosen to be wise

Dr. Ron B. Allen
*for putting me on the right track
in understanding this journal of Solomon*

—〰—

"There are more things in heaven
and earth, Horatio,
than are dreamt of in *your* philosophy."

—*William Shakespeare*

Contents

—◆—

Acknowledgements

—ɯ—

Karen Williams
for the initial editing and proofing

Kristen and Shirley Brewer
for your thoughts, notes, and encouragement

Joy Daugherty
for re-reading and formatting

Kristina Bubar, Sean Johnson, and C. J. Bergma
for their insights regarding wisdom in worship
(Ecclesiastes 5:1-7)

Foreword

—⟋⟍⟍—

*K*ohelet is a non-linear, authentic, down-to-earth and, at times, disturbing author. Although initially penned approximately three thousand years ago, *Ecclesiastes* could easily pass as the latest work by some trendy post-modern author. It is philosophical, yet practical; sacred, but raw. While it is a very spiritual book, it is most definitely not your typical *religious* book nor does it fit the stylistic mold of a systematic theologian. One Bible commentator referred to it as the "black sheep of the Bible." Another says, "It meanders, with jumps and starts, through the general messiness of human experience, to which it is a response."[1] Within the Bible, Ecclesiastes is a member of the wisdom books, meaning that it offers advice for succeeding in life, somewhat of an ancient self-help book. Yet, in other ways, it is like reading a diary or a prayer journal. *But not just any journal!* Kohelet has the unique reputation of being the world's "wisest man," a sage for the ages. Yet, in spite of this distinction, he openly struggles with life's absurdities, *and* he's willing to talk about it.

In my opinion, Ecclesiastes is the most philosophical of the biblical manuscripts. Kohelet tells us that it was his goal in life to "study and to probe with wisdom all that happens under the sun" (1:13). Maintaining his belief in God, he acknowledges the injustices of life, its mysteries, and the limitations of human knowledge and yet, he refuses to offer sugary or pat answers to these disturbing issues. He is absolutely determined to discover truth. Initially he does look to Scripture or tradition for guidance but, like most of us, whether consciously or unconsciously, he strives to discover truth through experience and individual reason.

Furthermore, he has arrived at some of his conclusions via non-sacred methods. He has not lived a perfect and holy life and yet, he is a biblical author. Nonetheless, when all is said and done, he delivers. He bares his soul. As a result of his transparency and vulnerability, he provides the reader with valuable wisdom and godly direction for living in confusing (dare I say postmodern?) times. *—Dr. Bobby Brewer*

Introduction

—∿∿—

Possibly you have read the title or the foreword and recoiled with, "What in the world is Kohelet?" The answer has to do with life. Life starts out pretty simple for most of us. Some of the biggest problems we faced as children were, "Why can't I have a ten-speed instead of a three-speed bike?" or "Why do I have to go to bed by seven?" But then our dog dies, and we never can get a good answer to our question, "Where did Bowzer go?" "Is Bowzer in heaven?" *"What happened to Bowzer?"* In Junior high our hormones went crazy, and in high school the social pressures beat us up pretty badly. After high school many of us experimented with a vast array of formulas for finding happiness in life and achieving the American dream. Along the way we developed a widening number of unanswered questions about life and its purpose. Sometimes we choose to ignore these mysteries, but at times they haunt our innermost being.

In the busyness of it all, we have the potential of losing touch with whom and what we are. How do you view yourself? A taxi for the kids? The provider for the family? Or someone who is just surviving and trying to make it! Speaking of which—make it to *what* exactly? Thus, some experience the proverbial "mid-life crisis" in which, somewhere in our forties or fifties, we conclude that if this is all life offers, we're going for the gusto!

It's been said that life begins simple and moves to the complex and then, if we do not learn how to press onto the "Profound Simple," we tend to become simplistic in our view of living. What exactly is this "Profound Simple?" Essentially it means that when we take another look at life, we decide what is really important to us. We eventually determine what really matters and satisfies our deepest desire to live; and whatever isn't important and doesn't matter, we neglect or abandon. The dilemma is to determine *what* to pursue and what to abandon. What pursuits will we ultimately discover to be phantoms that sooner or later result in disappointment, maybe even disaster? Where are we going to find the answers to these kinds of questions? How can you know with absolute certainty? Who knows? The answer is Kohelet!

CHAPTER 1

Who Is Kohelet?

—ᚱ—

Not to be confused with *Kabbalah* or any of the Eastern religions, Kohelet does, indeed, have roots in the Ancient Near East, the land of Israel. Furthermore, Kohelet's writings are considered sacred and are found within the pages of the Hebrew Scriptures also known as the Old Testament. Specifically, Kohelet is a part of the collection of books within the Bible known as the *Wisdom Writings*.

What Are the Wisdom Writings?

Hebrews 1:1 says, "God spoke through the prophets in many portions and in many ways." God communicated with his people in at least three different ways. First, he spoke through priests, specifically through Moses in the Torah (the first five books of the Bible).[1] Second, he spoke through the prophets. Third, he spoke through the counsel of the sages. These were wise men who observed and examined life and, under the inspiration of God, would extrapolate what was called *hokma,* or wisdom, the skill of living. Wisdom was a way of looking at life from the perspective of experiencing it in contrast to direct revelation. The wisdom writings of the Old Testament were divided into what I call *Affirmative Wisdom* and *Acceptive Wisdom*.

- *Affirmative Wisdom* is found predominately in the Psalms, Song of Songs, and Proverbs. It is when one can begin to figure out and understand how God's world works and how you can become successful at living in it.
- *Acceptive Wisdom* is contained in the books of Job and Kohelet. This is that paradox, that tension, of life. The fact is, we cannot always figure it out and understand how God's world works. At times it doesn't make a whole lot of sense! For example:

Why do bad things happen to good people?
Why do the innocent suffer while the wicked prosper?
Why do evil people get rich?
Why does it seem that the wrong people are
running the world?
Why is it that wanted felons never seem to get hit
by a drunk driver?
Where are the real and lasting pleasures of life?
Why does life get boring at times when we have so much?
Why do the rich and famous take their own lives?

Picture yourself with a cup coffee, sitting at a cozy café, and listening to a wise old man who has had it all, lived it all, experienced it all, and who is now ready to tell you the truth about it all. Compound this with the fact that his wisdom is world-renowned and people from all over the world have come to seek his counsel. His name is Kohelet.

Seven times this man is referred to by this name in the Bible. You, of course, are probably more familiar with the Greek translation of his name: *Ecclesiastes*.

The Preacher

The title of the book comes from the name of the character who is speaking. Technically, the Hebrew word *kohelet* is used to refer to a member of the assembly who teaches publicly, a preacher. The word *Ecclesiastes* is the Greek word for "Preacher" but the actual Hebrew word is *Kohelet*." The English translation of "Preacher" is a bit misleading because we think of someone giving a sermon. However, within its context, the setting is that of an assembly of wise sages who have gathered together for the specific purpose of hearing the final discourse on the meaning of life by the wisest of them all — Kohelet.

The story goes that a famous modern abstract artist was asked to explain one of his oil paintings. Specifically, he was asked what he was trying to communicate in one particular painting. "When I finished painting this picture, I stepped back and it didn't say anything to me. Then I turned it on its side, and still it didn't say anything to me. So, I turned the picture upside down, and that was what I wanted to say!"

Kohelet, however, does not paint upside down pictures. He is very clear, painfully clear, as to what he means to say, and he communicates it right side up! Furthermore, this is his final gift. Basically, like a baton, he is passing on this gift of wisdom given to him by God. So, who exactly is this man?

The Author

He has already given us a clue in the very first verse of the first chapter. This is King Solomon, *The* Solomon. Solomon was the wealthiest monarch that Israel would ever know (1 Kings 3:12; 5:9-14), and due to the divided kingdom after his death, he was the only "son of David" to rule over all of Israel. "I, the Preacher, have been king over Israel in Jerusalem" (Eccl. 1:12). Solomon was given the gift of wisdom that exceeded the wisdom of all others (1 Kings 3:10-12). In addition to wisdom, Solomon was provided with the wealth to do it all—and he did, including foolishness and imprudence. He would become imprudent and mishandle nearly everything that had been given to him. God, however, is no respecter of persons, and even Solomon would experience God's discipline (1 Kings 11:9, 14, 23). We read in 1 Kings 11:41 that the book of *Ecclesiastes* is the reflections of the aged and disciplined Solomon. We read what he learned from his wisdom about life: the good, the cultured, and the Profound Simple. "[God said,] behold I have done according to your words. Behold, I have given you a wise and discerning heart, so that there has been no one like you before, nor shall one like you arise after you. I have also given you what you have not asked, both riches and honor, so that there will not be any among the kings like you all your days" (1 Kings 3:12-13).

Why Kohelet?

The ancient Rabbinic schools debated whether or not this book would "defile the hands." Like *Song of Solomon*, parts of it are a bit embarrassing. This is because, at first glance, it does come across a bit pessimistic and negative (Eccl. 1:2, 17-18; 2:11, 19-20; 6:12; 7:15-16; 9:4-5). "Vanity! Vanity! ... All is vanity." "It's all meaninglessness!" These sound like the remarks of a Jean Paul Sartre, Albert Camus, or some French intellectual, not something you'd find within the pages of the Holy Bible. However, the book isn't pessimistic at all. Rather, it's intended to advocate how to live a fulfilling life. Raw honesty doesn't have to equate to pessimism. Seventeen times in this book you find the word *simhah*, the Hebrew root for "gladness" and "pleasure" along with its verb form *samah* meaning to "rejoice." Laced throughout the book you have statements like:

- "There is nothing better for a man than to eat and drink and tell himself that his labor is good" (2:24).

- "I know that there is nothing better for them than to rejoice and to do good in one's lifetime. Moreover, that every man who eats and drinks sees good in all his labor—it is the gift of God" (3:12-13).
- "I have seen that nothing is better than that man should be happy in his activities, for that is his lot" (3:22).
- "Enjoy life with the woman whom you love all the days of your fleeting life, which He has given to you under the sun, for this is your reward in life and in your toil in which you have labored under the sun" (7:9).
- "Go then, eat your bread in happiness and drink your wine with a happy heart; for God has already approved your works" (9:7).

What is Solomon saying to us? Where is he going with all of this? We are provided with insight to this in both the preface and the conclusion of the book. Kohelet's preface is given in 1:2, "Vanity of vanities," says the Preacher.

"Vanity of vanities! All is vanity." "Vanity" is the key word to the entire book. Five times it is used in this verse alone. Our English word "vanity" is actually not the best of translations because in today's English, "vain" is typically thought of as "meaningless" which implies that the message of the book is that life is meaningless. For example, even the *New International Version* translates it: "'Meaningless! Meaningless!' says the Teacher. 'Utterly Meaningless! Everything is Meaningless.'" This, however, is *not* the message of the book! The Hebrew word is *hevel*, which means, "vapor" or "breath." (See also Psalms 39:5,6,11; 61:9; 144:4; and Job 7:16.) If you've ever studied another language, you know that sometimes it can be difficult to capture the meaning of some words in the translation process. Although initially English words like "steam" and "vapor" do not seem to help—it does when we realize that "vapor" is not meaningless. Like "steam" it can be wasted or it can be used. Consider, for example, its use in Psalm 39:5: "Behold, you have made my days as handbreadths, and my lifetime as nothing in you sight; surely every man at his best is a mere *breath*" (emphasis mine). The usage of *hevel* conveys a brief and transitory status. Because life is a vapor (Jas. 4:14), sometimes it appears to be a futile attempt to try to make sense of it all.

This, however, is the value of Kohelet. Consider the epilogue of 12:9, "In addition to being a wise man, the Preacher [Kohelet] also taught the people knowledge; and he pondered, searched out and arranged many proverbs." Thus, these are not the words of a bitter, pessimistic old man. Rather, they are that of a wise man teaching us wisdom, even being careful and selective with the use of his words. We are told in 12:10 that "the Preacher sought to find delightful words and to write words of truth *correctly*" (emphasis mine).

Verse 12:11 adds that he has searched for "good words," and that these words are *yosher*, Hebrew for "straight" or "inerrant"! He admits that they are "goads"—sharp words to prod us out of the haze of a mishandled life. We are told what we *need* to hear and not necessarily what we *want* to hear. These words are "well-driven nails," like pegs on a wall on which to hang something heavy or important, or to fasten permanently. They are words that will stand the pressure of real life. Because Solomon was inspired by God to pen this ancient manuscript, "The Shepherd," that is God Himself, ultimately gives these words to us. Obviously, this is why Ecclesiastes is in the Bible!

Ancient Secrets Revealed

Ecclesiastes is Acceptive Wisdom—trying to make sense out of an apparent senseless world—trying to put it all together with all its contradictions and enigmas along with the challenge of acquiring it before life passes us by like a vapor. Does that mean life is senseless and, therefore, meaningless? It may pass by too fast for any of us to figure it out, but not for the eternal *God* who created it. A life based on God's wisdom is one that will not be lived in vain.

Consider the following ancient secrets revealed to us through Kohelet:

- God is wise and has a plan even when we can't always figure it out (3:11; 7:14; 8:17).
- God is good and life is a good gift from him (3:12, 13).
- God is just and shall reward the good and judge the wrongs that have been done (3:16-17; 8:11-13).

Thus, as you can see, Kohelet is actually emphasizing a point: the preciousness of life; *Carpe Diem*. Enjoy the good of creation now for it passes quickly like a vapor. Seize the moment of life! Life is a good gift from the hand of God.

CHAPTER 2

The Enigma of Pursuit
Ecclesiastes 1:1-11

—⟋⟍⟋—

In the previous chapter, we began with an overview of what Solomon wants us to understand about the real world. Clearly, the intent of the author is not to destroy our hope in this life but rather to help us understand how life "under the sun" is lived *if* it is to be enjoyed and maximized. As we trace this wisdom throughout the book, Dr. Walt Kaiser reveals that the flow is made up of four sections.

1. Life is given by God as a gift to enjoy (1:1--2:26).
2. God has a plan for accomplishing this (3:1--5:20).
3. God explains the plan (6:1--8:15).
4. God then applies that plan to our lives (8:16--12:14).

Although life is given as a gift to enjoy, there is something keeping us from tapping into the enjoyment. Solomon tells us it's a distracting restlessness that haunts us, causing us to be in constant motion, leading us nowhere.

The Preface, 1:1-2

"The words of the Preacher, the son of David, king in Jerusalem. 'Vanity of vanities,' says the Preacher, 'Vanity of vanities! All is vanity'" (Eccl. 1:1-2). "The words of the Preacher"—remember this is Kohelet, Solomon, the wisest of all sages sharing the meaning of life. Although technically the phrase, "the son of David," could refer to any of his descendants, Solomon, in addition to being the last king to rule over a united Israel (Eccl. 1:12), was unique among all other descendants of David in that he had been given the gift of wisdom and the wealth to be able to explore life with it. (See Eccl. 2:10; 12:9. See also 1 Kings 4:29-34; 12:9.)

Vanity of Vanities, All Is Vanity. This preface statement is a key to the message of the book, and a failure to properly grasp the meaning will result in missing the point altogether. The word "vanity" is utilized over thirty times in this book, and its primary meaning is "vapor" or "breath." Its repetition in Ecclesiastes is meant to emphasize a theme.[1] In other words, if the Hebrew writer wanted us to grab onto something important, he would emphasize it by continually repeating it. When an author added a plural, "vanity of vanities,"[2] the emphasis was taken even further. "Vapor of vapors, the thinnest of all vapors."

Life passes so quickly, like a vapor, that to fully comprehend its true purpose is futile. This concept is not limited to the Hebrew Scriptures but is also evidenced in the New Testament: "Why, you do not even know what will happen tomorrow. What is your life? You are a mist that appears for a little while and then vanishes" (Jas. 4:14).

The Question, 1:3

"What advantage does a man have in all his work?" (Eccl. 1:3). This is the biggest question of the whole book. This word "advantage" (*yitron*) is better translated "profit." It was a Hebrew commercial term found in Scripture exclu-

sively in Ecclesiastes. It refers to what's left over for enjoyment. Basically, the question is: "What's in it for me?" Do you want to receive some return for your investment into living? Do you feel you are getting out of life what you put into it? Take a minute to consider some real dilemmas:

- The businessman who strived to build an estate his whole life only to have his financial fortunes reversed and lost in his twilight years;
- Social activists who spend their lives to change laws only to see them overturned under the direction of a new leader;
- A frugal homemaker battling the undefeatable second law of thermo dynamics in her home;
- The scientists who spend their lives trying to discover new formulas for improving the world, only to see others utilizing their discoveries to pollute, damage, and destroy what they had wanted to enhance.

What is the enduring profit for living life so daily? After all of the energy and time that is spent towards a "constant motion," what exactly is the fruit? As Kohelet asks in 1:3, "What advantage does man have in all his work which he does under the sun?" Not to be overlooked, Kohelet utilizes this phrase "under the sun" twenty-nine times. This wisdom of Solomon in this journal has to do within the context of life on this planet, mortal living as designed by God to be enjoyed. He's talking about from birth to the grave. He's not talking about a life hereafter—not yet.

Living Under the Sun, 1:4-11

"A generation goes and a generation comes, but the earth remains forever" (Eccl. 1:4).

Life can be boring. Pre-medieval philosophers often speculated and theorized about the four elements that made up the universe: earth, air, fire, and water. Kohelet utilizes these as an analogy from the observable world to illustrate the point.[3]

Look at the Earth (Eccl. 1:4). "A generation goes and a generation comes, but the earth remains forever." In some ways it seems a bit ironic that humanity was made to rule the planet and yet, it's the planet that persistently endures. Most of us, however, will not live to see our eighty-fifth birthday. Jerome saw this same irony when he wrote: "What is vainer than this vanity: That the earth, which was made for humans, stays—but humans themselves, the Lords of the earth suddenly dissolve into dust?"

The Message translates Ecclesiastes 1:4, "One generation goes its way, the next one arrives, but nothing changes—it's business as usual for old planet earth." Life is like that; temporary" (transitory, transient, short-lived, fleeting, short-termed, impermanent, momentary, here today and gone tomorrow).

Look at the Sun (Eccl. 1:5). "Also, the sun rises and the sun sets; and hastening to its place it rises there again. The sun "hastens" to its place. The writer poetically gives human emotions to our sun. Literally, he is saying "the sun pants" in exhaustion to get where it goes only to return again. Kohelet uses the sun to illustrate what we would refer to as "the rat race." This is the "dailyness" of life. After being exhausted, I must undertake the whole ordeal again, the monotonous repetition of labor. Life is like that, repetitive, monotonous, tedious, boring, mundane, tiresome, and recurring.

Look at the Wind (Eccl. 1:6). "Blowing toward the south, then turning toward the north, the wind continues swirling along; and on its circular courses the wind returns."

The reference to the wind illustrates its erratic and unpredictable nature. In the desert, the wind moves sand dunes back and forth, always changing but never really accomplishing anything. There is no purpose nor is there a pattern.

Rather, it appears to be an aimless venture. Life is like that—"aimless"—purposeless, goalless, haphazard.

Look at the Rivers (Eccl. 1:7) "All the rivers flow into the sea, yet the sea is not full. The place where the rivers flow, there they flow again." This is another example of apparent pointless activity. Countless streams and rivers flow into the ocean without ever filling it. Perhaps, he may have also had the Dead Sea in mind. There are no outlets from the Dead Sea and yet, it has three rivers flowing into it: the Jordan, Arnon, and the Zered. Nonetheless, the Dead Sea never fills up. There is that constant motion of futility, never accomplishing anything. Life is like that…"futile."

Solomon is describing a *restlessness* in the human soul, the feeling that life is *transient, aimless, repetitive,* and *futile.* If we were going to sum up Solomon's words, we would say: "Life can be boring."

What Do We All Have in Common? 8-11

"All things are wearisome; Man is not able to tell it. The eye is not satisfied with seeing, nor is the ear filled with hearing" (Eccl. 1:8). According to Kohelet, what do the earth, sun, wind, and rivers have in common? Each is restless and in a "constant motion," accomplishing very little, if anything at all. Our eyes are not satisfied; our ears are never filled with hearing. No matter how beautiful to the eye or pleasing to the ear, we are only left with the desire for more. When we find things we like and enjoy, we rarely find ourselves saying, "Well that's enough for one lifetime." No matter how much, no matter how good or even how long, it will make little difference. We still crave for more. We may become satiated but never satisfied.

Here's the old news:
"That which has been is that which will be, and that which has been done is that which will be done. So there is nothing new under the sun. Is there anything of which one might say,"

See this, it is new"? Already it has existed for ages which were before us" (Eccl. 1:9-10).

Herodotus and Thucydides, ancient Greek Historians of the fifth century B.C., were concerned with the major problems of their day:

1. The threat of international war
2. The demise of marriage and rise of divorce
3. The rebellion of their youth and their apathetic attitude in following the counsel of their elders, preferring instead to embrace new fads
4. The corruption of politics and injustice within the courts
5. The terrible condition of the potholes in the public roads

What has history taught us? Apparently, not much! Consider the message of verse 11:

"There is no remembrance of earlier things; and also of the later things which will occur, there will be for them no remembrance among those who will come later still" (Eccl. 1:11).

Think of those who have gone before us and worked hard to give us a better world than what they had. While it may be easy to remember our grandparents' and even our great-grandparents' names, do we remember what they did and what they taught us about living life?

So the question is, "Why bother?" What's the *yitron*, the profit? What do we really achieve from all of our sweat, worry, and stress? Is it merely a constant motion that is transient, repetitive, aimless, and futile? Do we as humans never learn from those before us? This, of course, begs the questions: What can make life purposeful and satisfying? How can we break free from the "rat race" of monotonous futility? In the June 2005 issue of Christian Country Magazine, Amy

Grant says, "I have made a lot of music and done a lot of things, but I'll tell you, I agree with Ecclesiastes that it all feels sort of empty until I sing songs like these, ones with deep, deep meaning and truth."

Here are some contemplations. Where are some of the most obvious places that you can discover a fresh, focused, and purposeful motion towards the significant?

- If you are a parent, aside from the tangibles, what do you hope to leave for your children? Your great-grandchildren?
- Jesus introduced a new paradigm: spiritual family is just as important as biological family (Mark 3: 31-35); what do you hope to leave them?
- How can you make a lasting and positive impact on the lives of those around you right now?

CHAPTER 3

The Welt of Wisdom
Ecclesiastes 1:12-18

—ʍ—

When I was a child my mother regularly encouraged me to study hard so I would be smart and yet, she would then turn around and say I was "too smart for my britches." Western civilization places great value on education, but what exactly are we expecting from it? Perhaps you have convinced yourself that if you were just smarter and acquired more knowledge, life would become more rewarding. Obviously education can broaden horizons and has the potential to open doors; but Kohelet is also going to tell us that there is a dark side to knowledge and wisdom.

Most of us have a desire to know things. Consider our "How to…" books and seminars. Knowledge does have the premium of helping us to feel important. There is a belief in the human heart that if I know more than you, I will find greater acceptance and, since acceptance equals worth, I will experience greater importance. Maybe people will like having me around because I have something they want: what I know. We all want people to want us and so, perhaps, additional intelligence will result in more influence and greater importance, and I will experience all that life has to offer. That's the formula for getting the most out of living, right?

Solomon, the most intelligent and wisest man who ever lived, provides a rather rude awakening: *"In much wisdom there is much grief, and increasing knowledge results in increasing pain" (Eccl. 1:18)*.

As we have already learned, Solomon is demonstrating that life is a gift from God and given to enjoy. Enjoying life, however, requires wisdom—the secret of Kohelet. Wisdom is an art and like art, if you don't know how to brush the colors on the canvas, life will be gray. Wisdom is the art of living.

Take a closer look and notice something interesting in the text. Solomon switches from the third person: *"The words of the Preacher…"* (1:1), to the first person, "I, the Preacher…" Solomon now is extrapolating from his own experience as a wise sage. Remember how the wisdom writings differ from the other writings of Scripture (chapter 1 of this book)? Here God speaks to a sage about life as he is *living it out*.

In the previous chapter, we illustrated that life can be pretty boring and filled with constant, transient, repetitive, aimless motion of futility. We must figure out the reason for all the motion. Like a mystery novel in the likes of Sherlock Holmes, we have an agreed upon and obvious dilemma and now, together, we'll begin to search for a solution. Ecclesiastes 1:13-18 begins the process. However, he warns us about the process and provides a bit of a disclaimer because, eventually, like Solomon himself, we'll eventually learn the somewhat rude and sobering truths.

First, wisdom cannot change reality (1:13-15) and second, wisdom can cause great pain (1:16-18).

Wisdom Cannot Change Reality, 1:13-15
"And I set my mind to seek and explore by wisdom concerning all that has been done under heaven. It is a grievous task which God has given to the sons of men to

be afflicted with. I have seen all the works which have been done under the sun, and behold, all is vanity and striving after the wind. What is crooked cannot be straightened, and what is lacking cannot be counted" (Eccl. 1:13-15). Notice how in 1:13 (also in 1:17) Solomon says, *"I set my mind."* This literary form[1] serves as bookends to exhibit what he wants to say about learning.

The Hebrew does not have a word for "mind." The Hebrew rendering is, "I applied my heart." To Jewish thinking, the heart included all three functions: intelligence, emotion, and will. To give his heart meant to give his total self with all his thinking, his emotions, and his will. It meant his total being. "To seek" was to go after the breadth of all knowledge, and "to explore" was the depth of it all. He's saying, "I took the assignment of studying all 'that has been done under heaven' and everything there is within the human experience, and I went after it with everything I had." *"I looked most carefully into everything, searched out all that is done on earth. And let me tell you, there's not much to write home about" (Eccl. 1:13-14, The Message).*

Solomon says he would pursue this task by means of "wisdom" using all the skill, cleverness, creativity, and insight he had been given. He says this was a "grievous task which God has given to the sons of men to be afflicted with." Here's the question: Why would it be so grievous?

We are all curious to know why things are as they are. This is why we have theology, philosophy, psychology, and science. Here Kohelet tells us God has placed this curiosity in our nature (3:11). This journal is addressed to all the sons and daughters of Adam created by God. Thus, what he is saying is that God is the one who has given humanity that deep desire to discover why things are the way they are. This is good isn't it? Not necessarily.

Here, towards the end of his life, Solomon gives us an overview of what he has discovered. He says he had taken note of everything that transpired on earth that could be observed. The conclusion: Life is *hevel*, a vapor. Discouragingly, even the satisfaction of the discovery fades. It's like "striving after the wind." The picture he is providing for his readers is that of a shepherd trying to guide the wind or grabbing for something only to see it pass through their fingers. The thrill of discovery doesn't last long, like wind passing through your fingers or a passing fragrance enjoyed briefly.

Kohelet gives a proverb:[2] *"What is crooked cannot be straightened" (Eccl. 1:15a).* Wisdom will not change the reality of life. It can influence it, but not change it. Knowledge and information in and of themselves do not have the ability to permanently alter anything. *Honest* philosophy will ultimately always lead to despair.

Philosophers like Albert Camus, Jean Paul Sartre, and Friedrich Nietzsche have all been lionized as great thinkers for suggesting that life (and humanity) is meaningless. Nietzsche went so far as to say that the only real solution is suicide. In fact, this sense of hopelessness is a key component within postmodern thinking.[3] To the postmodernist, the twentieth century, for example, was anything but the utopia that was envisioned by the rational thinkers of the modern era. To quote one postmodern author, "Besides, what did Science, Reason and Progress get us, after all? The twentieth century turned out to be nothing; if not a dark, Kafkaesque nightmare of rationally administered death camps, death squads, Auschwitz, World Wars 1 and 2, Hiroshima, Nagasaki, ecological and disaster and various systems of totalitarianism. And all in the name of the Enlightenment values of Science, Reason, Liberation, Freedom and Progress."[4]

Dr. Paul Feyeraberd, professor of Philosophy at the University of California-Berkeley simply says, "Western ideals of progress are damaging sociologically and ecologically."[5]

Solomon's point is that knowledge is insufficient for improving the human condition. The twisted will remain twisted and the missing will resist human calculation. When he says, "What is lacking cannot be counted," he means there will always be things that fail to reach their full potential. Thus, the limit of wisdom and knowledge is the fact that regardless of how much information we acquire "under the sun," it does not provide nor guarantee the ability to change anything. So, perhaps you are asking: "How is knowing this going to help me enjoy life?"

The answer is, life must begin with raw truth, an accurate understanding of how it works. For example, consider how often we spend time trying to change people. Occasionally we may even succumb to manipulation or controlling behavior, but the raw truth is, we can't change them! When we come to this realization, life becomes simpler and more enjoyable. Likewise, think of all the conversations we've had in regard to global politics to "change the world." What changes in human nature and the nature of things have we seen? We can't change people! Likewise, we are not always able to even change things.

God is aware of this, and I am *not* suggesting that we shouldn't try—no not at all? Rather, we can make the most of this wisdom by becoming an influencer who understands that only God can actually bring about lasting and legitimate change. We can influence, and He makes the changes. With this we need only to be faithful in what we do and not get discouraged with the results, they are in His hands.

At some point in your life, you've probably heard of the "Serenity Prayer":

God grant me the serenity
to accept the things I cannot change,
courage to change the things I can,
and the wisdom to know the difference.

I believe that Kohelet would have liked this prayer because the prayer shows that the human condition can only change with the intervention of someone outside of it, someone who is not living "under the sun." Only God can change a person's heart. Therefore, we can stop trying to play the divine role! We influence, but only God changes.

"What is lacking cannot be counted"(Eccl. 1:15b). If we focus on what cannot be straightened or what is always missing or not right, we'll be wasting what little time we do have on earth. Remember, there are two kinds of wisdom spoken of in the Bible: "Affirmative" and "Acceptive." This is what the "Serenity Prayer" is all about. Change what you can but simultaneously have the wisdom to accept what you cannot change.

Wisdom Can Cause Great Pain, 1:16-18

"I said to myself, 'Behold, I have magnified and increased wisdom more than all who were over Jerusalem before me; and my mind has observed a wealth of wisdom and knowledge. And I set my mind to know wisdom and to know madness and folly; I realized that this also is striving after wind. Because in much wisdom there is much grief, increasing knowledge results in increasing pain" (Eccl. 1:16-18).

Solomon states that he had acquired more wisdom and knowledge, more than all of the previous rulers over Jerusalem.[6] The "knowledge" is information learned, and the "wisdom" is the skill of using it. Wisdom is making the connections in life, the connections between decisions and results, behavior and consequences. Notice he says, "I said to myself." In Hebrew this is translated as "I communed with my heart."[7] In 1:17, he closes the bracket by repeating: "And I set my mind; I applied my heart, my whole being to the task of knowing wisdom." This "wisdom" he is referring to is *hokmah*, known in the Bible as a great treasure to be gained and has the primary meaning of "skill" (i.e., to do something skillfully).

Dr. Fred Barshaw, a former principal at an inner city school in Los Angeles, used to share with me his frustration with the educational structure that tended to recognize only one kind of intelligence: book knowledge. Thus, academics were everything. God, however, has provided a vast array of intelligences other than book knowledge. For example, there is mechanical, musical, language, art, social and athletic intelligence. The word *hokmah* is a reference to all of the differing types of wisdoms given by God.

- Exodus 28:3: A skillful person in making a garment; "Hokmah of heart, I have given them the spirit of hokmah."
- Exodus 31:3-5: Craftsmanship and Art
- Exodus 35:26, 35: Embroidery and Spinning Goat Hair
- Exodus 36:1-2: Architects, Contractors, and Builders

Solomon counsels in Proverbs 22:6: "Train a child in the way he should go, and when he is old he will not turn from it." To train "in the way" means keeping in the way God has designed them. The word "way" speaks of his manner, i.e. his capacities for receiving wisdom. We also see this concept used in another Hebrew proverb: "There are three things that are too amazing for me, four that I do not understand: the way of an eagle in the sky, the way of a snake on a rock, the way of a ship on the high seas, and the way of a man with a maiden" (Prov. 30:18-19).

What if the Lord has given them a "wise heart" in something other than academics? Thus, we shouldn't limit wisdom to the "smart people" because wisdom transcends and is not dependant upon academic or intellectual intelligence. Some of the most foolish people I've seen claim to be "smart." This is not meant to sound pejorative, but I can truthfully attest to the fact that there have been occasions in which some of the more heartless people I have ever met possessed doctoral degrees (even in theology). Whereas some of the godliest and wisest people I have ever met never graduated from high school.

Just when we think everything is crystal clear, there is a disturbing twist in the plot. Solomon also says that he made it his objective to *also know madness and folly.* This is quite the paradox because we have the wisest man being deluded into believing there is satisfaction in the very things that ultimately produce destruction. He knew it was madness and that is the folly (idiocy). Like a modern day heroine addict, he knew he was being deceived but, to his own demise, pursued it anyway.

He discovered this to be "striving after wind." All the pleasures passed through his fingers and left him empty. This helps explain his final assessment in 1:18: "Much wisdom equals much grief. Increasing knowledge equals increasing pain." Solomon's frustration was not with the meaninglessness of life but with the inability to make sense out of what he could understand. Don't misunderstand—the point isn't that ignorance is bliss. Rather, he is saying that we may grow in wisdom and knowledge, but we ought to change one word, the word "in" to the word "with." We will grow *with* wisdom and knowledge because both are allies that will deepen and sharpen us as iron sharpens iron. "Pain" comes with knowledge because it deepens our sensitivity to the reality of life. Or as an old song puts it:

> *There's just one thing you need to know,*
> *and that is hurting only makes you grow.*
> *The pain you feel is the first step to being healed.*
> *There is just one thing you need to do*

and that is get your eyes off you.
Place them on the Lord
and he'll make pain an open door.

With learning comes the deeper insight into the many things that are wrong about our world. Enlightened eyes will see the injustice in society. There is pain when we come to the conclusion that we cannot change it. There is pain and suffering in life under the sun. God is sensitized to it and, in sensitizing us to it, He makes us more human.

There is a disease called Hansen's disease. One of its side effects is that it affects all the nerve endings of the body, causing you to no longer feel pain. The disease is better known as leprosy. Basically, what happens is that you begin to destroy yourself with more injuries because you can't feel the pain.

Don't be afraid of pain that's associated with learning. Like anyone, I fear disappointment and failure. But over the years I've also learned that on occasion, I've cultured some valuable lessons about life as a result of disappointment and failure.

The Apostle Paul understood this when he said, "I have learned to be content in whatever circumstances I am. I know how to get along with humble means and I also know how to live in prosperity; in any and every circumstance I have learned the secret of being filled and going hungry, both of having abundance and suffering need. I can do all things through him who strengthens me" (Phil. 4:11-13).

CHAPTER 4

The Enigma of Pleasure
Ecclesiastes 2:1-11

—◊◊◊—

Epicurus was a third-century Greek philosopher who summed up life as being the avoidance of pain and the pursuit of pleasure. Epicurus defined pleasure as simplicity, prudence, honor, and justice. Although most of us may not agree with his definition, I can certainly understand his premise. In psychology, for example, the "pleasure principle" is an informal term that refers to the automatic adjustment of the mental activity to secure pleasure or gratification and to avoid pain or unhappiness. For the average American, pleasure is simply having a good time…which is what exactly?

According to Webster's Dictionary, pleasure is enjoyment, delight, and satisfaction. As a Christian I wonder if it's even permissible to discuss something as hedonistic as pleasure. If the world avoids pain and pursues pleasure, then wouldn't it be more spiritual for us to avoid pleasure and pursue pain? Our monastic friends have committed their lives to this belief. Isn't pleasure evil? Not necessarily. The Bible says, "Every good thing bestowed and every perfect gift is from above, coming down from the Father of lights" (James 1:17). In the following section Kohelet provides his perspective on pleasure. Be careful not to second-guess him too soon.

A Pre-Conclusion About Pleasure, 2:1-3

"I said to myself, 'Come now, I will test you with plea-sure. So enjoy yourself.' And behold, it too was futility" *(Eccl. 2:1).*

Here again Kohelet has a communing-with-his-heart session; taking time for thought and asking himself all the hard questions about some of the things he enjoyed the most. Generally, we tend to avoid this. Remember how much more we enjoyed certain foods until we learned what they did to us (I miss chili dogs!). Recently I discovered that my favorite sweetener for my tea might affect my memory, yet I could die of a heart attack from being overweight...or perhaps I'll die from memory loss, forgetting to lose weight.

Solomon says to himself, "Self, I will test you." This is the same word used when God *tested* Abraham's faith with Isaac. *Nasah* means to prove something once and for all and, within this context, it is about pleasure. The word "pleasure" is a very broad term and speaks of everything from the simple delights of life to deeper passions. Solomon provides a preview of his conclusion and reveals that it too was "futility," a passing vapor.

However, *remember what futility meant?* It's another translation of the same word *hevel*. The essence here is that there is nothing of permanence in any of it. It passes quickly like a vapor through your fingers, a fragrance enjoyed in the moment.

"I said of laughter, 'It is madness,' and of pleasure, 'What does it accomplish?'" *(Eccl. 2:2).*

Why does Solomon say that laughter is madness? It's because, ultimately, it accomplishes nothing. Although grat-ifying for the moment, there is no real sustaining value in it. From the simple delights that give laughter to the passion, which when gratified give pleasure, there is the potential for great deception. We pursue these as goals of life and yet, what value is left over to enjoy the next day? Proverbs 14:13 says, "Even in laughter the heart may be in pain, and the end of joy may be grief."

"I explored with my mind how to stimulate my body with wine while my mind was guiding me wisely, and how to take hold of folly, until I could see what good there is for the sons of men to do under heaven the few years of their lives" *(Eccl. 2:3).* Or, as *The Message* puts it: *"What do I think of the fun-filled life? Insane! Insane. My verdict on the pursuit of happiness; who needs it? With the help of a bottle of wine and all the wisdom I could muster, I tried my level best to penetrate the absurdity of life. I wanted to get a handle on anything useful we mortals might do during the years we spend on this earth"* *(2:2-3).*

It's important to understand what Solomon *isn't* saying. He isn't saying that he went out and got bombed; but note that he says it was while his *mind was guiding him wisely.* The Hebrew rendering is "he drew out his flesh with wine." This means that he stimulated his senses not to excess but so that he could evaluate the sensations he was feeling. To many this sounds like I'm making an excuse for Solomon. I am not condoning drunkenness. That stated, it is insightful to understand the text as it was meant to be understood. Solomon wasn't a victim of alcohol but was very calculating in its use. Why do that? So he could *take hold* of "folly."

He says he was going to try all the "fun things" that men do for the few years they have under the sun. He would see for himself whether the promised pleasure that others raved about as being so enjoyable was real. He wanted to see if all the hype was authentic and if any of them were worthy of spending a lifetime pursuing. In 2:4-9, he will test three kinds of pleasure.

The Pursuit of Beauty, 2:4-6.

"*I enlarged my works: I built houses for myself, I planted vineyards for myself*" *(Eccl. 2:4).* It appears that Solomon enjoyed both the concept and the process of building beautiful homes. He devoted thirteen years to building his own house (1 Kings 7:1-12), and then he built "The House of the Forest Lebanon," another house for his wife, the Pharaoh's daughter. He also built *cities*: Hazor, Megiddo, Gezer, Beth-Horon, Baalath, and Tamar in the wilderness. Perhaps he is best known for building the Temple in Jerusalem, which is often referred to as Solomon's Temple. However, he couldn't take credit for its construction because it was a divine mandate and his father and predecessor, King David, provided most of the materials. He does mention planting "vineyards" and also appreciated the beauty of plants because he used them to describe the beauty of his bride, "My beloved is to me a cluster of henna blossoms in the vineyards of Engedi" (Song of Sol. 1:14).

"*I made gardens and parks for myself and I planted in them all kinds of fruit trees*" *(Eccl. 2:5).* He made gardens and parks for himself. Gardens come from *ganan* meaning "to guard." Gardens were enclosed areas that were "guarded" with flowers and fruit orchards. He loved these things (Song of Sol. 4:12-15; 6:2, 3, 11). Parks were open areas planted with forests and fruit trees containing herds of animals.[1] "My beloved has gone down to his garden, to the beds of balsam, to pasture his flock in the gardens and gather lilies" (Song of Sol. 6:2).

"*I made ponds of water for myself from which to irrigate a forest of growing trees*" *(Eccl. 2:6).* Reflective ponds in an arid land were a luxury and yet, in his wisdom, he used these same ponds for the irrigation of his gardens and parks. Typically, they were massive. One manmade pond found in the Valley of Artas has a length of 582 feet with a width of 207 feet and a depth of 50 feet. Multiple houses, numerous vineyards, luxurious gardens, and lush parks are examples of the esthetic beauty in Solomon's life. Additionally, he received the pleasure that comes from producing it and enjoying its beauty. Whether it's the pleasure we receive by making something beautiful or from simply enjoying the beauty of someone's work, these visual pleasures are esthetic.

The Pursuit of Prestige, 2:7
"I bought male and female slaves and I had home born slaves; also I possessed flocks and herds larger than all who preceded me in Jerusalem" (Eccl. 2:7).

The construction and maintenance of Solomon's various projects required a massive labor force; thus, he purchased slaves and even had slaves born into his household. In addition to being a culturally acceptable practice in the ancient Near East, prestige was also acquired by owning slaves. Solomon's possessions affected the senses of the Queen of Sheba (1 Kings 10:4-5). "When the Queen of Sheba perceived all the wisdom of Solomon, the house that he had built, the food at his table, the seating of his servants, the attendance of his waiters and their attire, his cupbearers, and his stairway by which he went up to the house of the Lord, there was no more spirit in her."

He possessed flocks and herds. If you want to know the numbers he is talking about, take the dedication sacrifices for the Temple: 22,000 oxen and 120,000 sheep (1 Kings 8:63), or take a look at one day's provisions for his household (1 Kings 4:22-23).[2] What is the pleasure of having possessions? In addition to the enjoyment of the beauty of things (esthetic pleasure), there is also the ego gratification of being able to possess the things that bring pleasure. However, there is also an ego pleasure in being envied and independent. The record of 2 Chronicles 1:14 tells us, "Solomon amassed chariots and horsemen. He had 1,400 chariots, and 12,000 horsemen...."

Flavius Josephus, a Jewish historian from the first century, writes the following in his *Antiquities of the Jews*: "Their riders also were a further ornament to them [Chariots], being in the first place, young men in the most delightful flower of their age, and being eminent for there largeness, and far taller than other men. They had also very long heads of hair hanging down, and were clothed in garments of Tyrian purple. They had also dust of gold every day sprinkled on their hair, so that their heads sparkled with the reflection of the sunbeams from the gold. The king himself rode upon a chariot in the midst of these men, who were still in armor and had their bows fitted to them."[3]

"Oh, how I prospered! I left all of my predecessors in Jerusalem far behind, left them behind in the dust. What's more, I kept a clear head through it all" (Eccl. 2:9, The Message).

Then there was…

The Pursuit of the Senses, 2:8-9

"Also, I collected for myself silver and gold and the treasure of kings and provinces I provided for myself male and female singers and the pleasures of men—many concubines" (Eccl. 2:8). To give you an idea of what he is talking about, hold your place here, get your Bible and take a moment to read 1 Kings 10:14-25. It is noteworthy that the "Treasures of Kings" were rare and special tributes given only to kings by other kings or royalty. 2 Chronicles 1:15 says, "The king made silver and gold as common in Jerusalem as stones and cedar as plentiful as sycamore trees in the foothills" (*NIV*). 1 Kings 10:25 also tells us that singers were brought in, both male and female, to make music and provide pleasure for his ears. Solomon wrote over one thousand songs himself (1 Kings 4:32).

The last part of verse 8, after "pleasures of men," seems obvious, but this last phrase has been translated differently in

the more popular versions. Whereas the King James Version
(*KJV*) translated it as "musical instruments," the *NASB* and
English Standard Version (*ESV*) translate it as "many concubines"; *The New International Version* (*NIV*) chose "harem"
and *The Message*, a paraphrase, took the liberty to say,
"Voluptuous maidens for my bed." The Hebrew is *shiddah
weshiddot*, which means *many* concubines. How many? 1
Kings 4:34 says that he had a thousand women to attend him
anytime for whatever he had in mind.[4]

*"Then I became great and increased more than all who
preceded me in Jerusalem. My wisdom also stood by me"
(Eccl. 2:9)*. Thus, every sensual pleasure which could be
experienced, he experienced! Remarkably, in spite of all
of this, his wisdom stayed with him. He did not forget the
task. Do all these pleasures, esthetic pleasure for the eyes,
ego pleasure for the pride and sensual pleasure for the flesh
satisfy and provide fulfilling and lasting enjoyment? The
Apostle John talks about these pleasures in 1 John 2:16-17.
"For all that is in the world, the lust of the flesh and the lust
of the eyes and the boastful pride of life, is not from the
Father, but is from the world. The world is passing away,
and also its lusts; but the one who does the will of God lives
forever." The desire for these pleasures has been around for
a long time (Gen. 3:6).

The Conclusion About Pursuing Pleasure, 2:10-11

*"All that my eyes desired I did not refuse them. I did
not withhold my heart from any pleasure, for my heart was
pleased because of all my labor and this was my reward for
all my labor" (Eccl. 2:10)*. How would you like to have that in
your testimony? He draws his conclusion and, as I said at the
beginning, don't be too quick to second-guess him on this.

Regardless of how vain or foolish it was, Solomon
did not deny himself any known gratification. However,
some pleasures produce misery and potentially result in

pain and destruction. That's why he referred to some pleasures as "madness and folly," pleasures that could delude
us into believing they would be lasting enjoyments but in
reality would result in great disappointment. Nonetheless,
Solomon's basic point is that he received his reward for his
labor—immediate pleasure. As usual, the pleasure typically
lasted only as long as the act itself or until the novelty of it
wore off.

God has given us the capacity to enjoy the sensations
of pleasure, "For everything created by God is good, and
nothing is to be rejected if it is received with gratitude" (1
Tim. 4:4), but how do we know which will produce genuine
enjoyment and which will produce pain?

*"Thus I considered all my activities which my hands
had done and the labor which I had exerted, and behold all
was vanity and striving after wind and there was no profit
under the sun" (Eccl. 2:11).* The enigmatic dilemma of the
enjoyment was that the pleasure passed quickly and slipped
through the fingers leaving nothing but a memory or a longing.
Thus, it was "vanity" and striving after the wind. Solomon
says, "There is no profit under the sun." It is now helpful to
remember the beginning of the book where he says, *"What
advantage does man have in all his work, which he does under
the sun?" (Eccl. 1:3).* What is the *yitron*? After the pleasure,
what is left to enjoy? Where is the lasting satisfaction? Or am
I left again with that empty feeling of a void?

The warning here is that we have a "Distraction Problem."
The temptation is to focus exclusively on the gift without
acknowledging the gift Giver. It is in the acknowledge-
ment of the gift Giver that we find the ultimate enjoyment
of the gift. The concept of delayed gratification is not a very
popular one. Rather, we are tempted to find the quick fix for
our immediate gratification. As a result, we may end up sacri-
ficing the ultimate gift which is the enjoyment of the rewards
of life that God has given us (Matt. 6:31-34). This secret of

Kohelet is in experiencing the pleasure we were all created to enjoy. Blaise Pascal was right when he said that "there is a God-shaped vacuum in every life that only God can fill." All of humanity is on a quest to fill this vacuum with something; but even though we try to fill it with every type and kind of pleasure imaginable, it is a vacuum that only God can fill. It will be in further-revealed wisdom that Solomon will tell us how this vacuum is filled with enjoyment.

CHAPTER 5

The Gift of Life
Ecclesiastes 2:12-26

—〰—

The story goes that a young friend of philosopher Bertrand Russell noticed that the celebrated thinker was in a state of deep and profound thought. The young man asked, "Why are you so meditative?" Russell replied, "Because I've made an odd discovery. Every time I talk to a savant [a learned scholar], I feel quite sure that happiness is no longer a possibility. Yet when I talk to my gardener, I'm convinced of the opposite."

When it comes to chasing, we are all chasing something and usually it has something to do with happiness. No one really wants to be miserable. Despite how some Christians may look or act, God has *not* called us to misery. The Bible, in fact, says just the opposite (Matt. 5:3-12). Most would agree with the premise that people want to be happy; the disagreement comes with the formula to happiness.

In *People* Magazine, B. F. Skinner said, "What arouses fear is not death itself, but the act of talking and thinking about it, and that can be stopped. We brood about death most when we have nothing else to do. The more reason we have to pay attention to life, the less time we have for attention to death. A properly executed will can give you the satisfaction of knowing your possessions will go to the right people, and you can extend the life of part of yourself by donating any organs that might still be useful. When those things have been done, it is probably better not to think about death."[1] How depressing. Is that his best counsel?

In our pursuit for happiness, maybe before we set our hearts on attaining something we think will bring it, perhaps we should look around and see how fulfilled it has made those who seemingly have it. Kurt Cobain outwardly had everything a typical guy could want. As the leader of a famous rock group, Pearl Jam, he unintentionally launched a new style of music and dress known as "grunge." He had a best-selling album, a lucrative record deal, was considered by many to be a musical genius, and seemingly was on top of the world, and yet, he ended his own life. Death seems to strike the final blow on any sort of lasting happiness. It doesn't seem to make any difference how smart you are or how much you have accomplished; the mortality rate is still 100 percent. Death knocks the pinions right out of wisdom and wealth.

As one commentator said, "If, as we might put it, every card in our hand will be trumped, does it matter how we play?" If that is the case, we are left with a question in the form of a syllogism.[2] If death renders wisdom futile, and if death robs labor of its fruit, then what is the gift of living anyway?

The Pursuit of Wisdom, 2:12-17

"So I turned to consider wisdom, madness and folly; for what will the man do who will come after the king except what has already been done?" (Eccl. 2:12). "So I turned..." Solomon now examines what he has observed in his life regarding what has been significant and meaningful and what hasn't. Interestingly, the "wisest man of all time" states

that wisdom itself came up short (1:12-18). Even if you can understand life, you're still unable to alter it. The acquisition of more information can result in more disappointments which can then increase our frustration and disappointment. So, you might be asking, "What's the solution?"

Solomon takes another look. He first compares wisdom with madness and folly. Madness is the delusion, whereas folly is in knowing better. He's in a legitimate place to make such deductions because he had "done it all." Any future endeavors will be futile repetitions of what Solomon has already experienced because, they too will ultimately reach the same conclusions.

"And I saw that wisdom excels folly as light excels darkness. The wise man's eyes are in his head, but the fool walks in darkness. And yet I know that one fate befalls them both." *(Eccl. 2:13-14)*. There is a difference between wisdom and folly. It is as different as light from darkness. The *yitron* (profit) of wisdom is the enjoyment of knowing that the pleasure is a reward of your labor from the hand of God. But the *yitron* of madness and folly is the pain and frustration that follows; the sting that follows the pleasure sensations. The wise man makes fewer mistakes; his "eyes are in his head," not in his glands. I have always said wisdom is the accumulation of "I'm not going to do that again!"

When you walk in darkness you don't know where you are going, and the result is that you do more damage to yourself than good. The wise, however, are going to be more successful in life. Nevertheless, whether successful or unsuccessful, there is still a shadow that hovers over both the wise and the foolish: they are both going to die! This is the sobering truth. No matter how great a life you have had, it all passes away. Furthermore, it is quick. "You are just a vapor," says James (4:14). Thus, one answer to the question, "Why does God let the good die young and the bad live on?" is that they both still die! A longer life does not necessarily mean a happier or more meaningful one.

"Then I said to myself, 'As is the fate of the fool, it will also befall me. Why then have I been extremely wise?' So I said to myself, 'This too is vanity'" (Eccl. 2:15). He asks himself an honest question here. Why be wise, why work so hard, what's the use of it if it's all only going to pass away like a vapor (*hevel*). If, like the fool, I am also going to die, what's the purpose of trying to be wise?

"For there is no lasting remembrance of the wise man as with the fool, inasmuch as in the coming days all will be forgotten and how the wise man and the fool alike die!" *(Eccl. 2:16).* Ultimately, no one is going to remember the difference anyway. However, in Ecclesiastes it's essential to always remember the under-the-sun concept (mortal life). Hebrews 6:10-12 teaches that there is *something* to be remembered. However, for this life, both the wise and the fool's memory go into oblivion. So he says "I hated life…" This seems out of place for the Bible, but please read on.

"So I hated life, for the work which had been done under the sun was grievous to me; because everything is futility and striving after wind" *(Eccl. 2:17).* What is this? The prime root of the Hebrew word here is *not* the one for emotion, but the one for choice. The Hebrew word for love (*Ahav*) spoke of the worth and value of something. Within this context, "hate" speaks of its opposite, *indifference*. Life no longer satisfies…I'm bored! This is similar to the proverbial "midlife crisis" that some struggle with in our contemporary culture. All of the goals are met, and then we ask ourselves, "Now what?"

From a different perspective, I wonder how Solomon felt when he realized that he was never going to attain fulfillment through his "pleasure experiments." I speculate that many in his shoes would have responded with deep depression. Solomon, however, doesn't respond this way. Why? Stay tuned. Meanwhile, he tells us that life was "grievous to me" and that it caused more pain than it was worth. Once again he says, "Everything is futility and striving after wind." It's impossible to make sense out of all of it because it passes so quickly!

This is why the seventeenth-century philosopher, Blaise Pascal, said that we try to keep ourselves so busy and pre-occupied: "Nothing is so insufferable to man as to be completely at rest, without passions, without business, without diversion, without study. He then feels his nothingness, his forlornness, his insufficiency, his independence, his weakness, his emptiness, there will immediately arise from the depth of his heart weariness, gloom, sadness, fretfulness, vexation and despair."

Death not only renders wisdom futile, but it also renders everything that is produced in us as futile. "But God said to him, 'Fool! This night your soul is required of you, and the things you have prepared, whose will they be? So is the one who lays up treasure for himself and is not rich toward God" (Luke 12:20-21).

But with death comes serious clarity about life.

The Pursuit of the Fruit of Your Labor, 2:18-23

"Thus I hated all the fruit of my labor for which I had labored under the sun, for I must leave it to the man who will come after me" (Eccl. 2:18). All Solomon had produced would ultimately be left for someone else. I have to admit that I too had thoughts of my sons pawning off my library to buy a ... motorcycle. As the saying goes, *you can't take it with you.* There will be no U-Haul trailers following your funeral procession. Yes, but shouldn't we strive to build up an estate to leave to our children and grandchildren? The question to ponder is does that inheritance breed gratefulness or greediness in my offspring?

"And who knows whether he will be a wise man or a fool? Yet he will have control over all the fruit of my labor for which I have labored by acting wisely under the sun. This too is vanity" (Eccl. 2:19). Like Solomon, unfortunately, we do not know with absolute certainty the character of the one who will be in control of all that we have worked for. Perhaps you are saying to yourself, "But you don't know my family." *Really?* We are no longer surprised at the relatives and "friends of the family" who respond when it comes to an inheritance? How many families do you know who still harbor bitterness over what happened? Where is everything that your grandparents owned? Who knows? It's up in the air. Who can be certain?

"Therefore I completely despaired of all the fruit of my labor for which I had labored under the sun. When there is a man who has labored with wisdom, knowledge and skill, then he gives his legacy to one who has not labored with them. This too is vanity and a great evil" (Eccl. 2:20-21). Again I turned to take another look at it all, and it didn't look so good. The issue is not the misuse of the inheritance but rather the fact that those who would receive it did not work for it. In organizational management, the aristocratic era is the most dangerous era for an organization because it means that the current leaders inherited all of the benefits of their predecessors but not the blood, sweat, and tears. Thus, there is no vested interest nor necessarily a belief in the original vision of the predecessor(s). There are plenty of great examples of those who were great and wise stewards of their inheritance. Likewise, you're probably aware of the spoiled-rich-child syndrome where there is no sense of reward, no sense of enjoying the fruit of their own labor. Solomon calls this "a great evil." Why? Remember in 2:10, he said that in spite of all of his experiments in the realm of pleasure, the one thing in which he found great delight was his work. Yet, we dream of winning the lottery. Our motto is to make more

and work less. Why? We are all greatly influenced by our culture and our pre-Christian beliefs, probably more than we realize. But the "get rich quick" or better yet the "get rich quick with no work" concept is actually a distortion of God's design for a man enjoying the reward of his labor from the hand of God.

Is it possible to leave an inheritance to our children without destroying their opportunity of enjoying the fruit of their labor? Yes, but it requires a great deal of training, discretion, and wisdom. Although we can have the best of intentions, this can very easily result in the wrong outcome. The Bible tells us in Proverbs 13:22, "A good man leaves an inheritance to his children's children"; and, therefore, we also do not want to live out what I saw on a bumper sticker on the back of a Winnebago that read, "We're spending our kid's inheritance."

"For what does a man get in all his labor and in his striving with which he labors under the sun? Because all his days his task is painful and grievous; even at night his mind does not rest. This too is vanity" (Eccl. 2:22-23). Pain and frustration are par for the course of life. Occasionally, stress even robs us of our sleep. For example, sometimes our thoughts about work or the day ahead prevent us from getting a good night's rest. So, once again, this begs the question: What is the gift of life?

The Pursuit of Life, 2:24-26

"There is nothing better for a man than to eat and drink and tell himself that his labor is good. This also I have seen, that it is from the hand of God" (Eccl. 2:24). Interestingly, both the Prophet Isaiah (22:13) and the Apostle Paul (1 Cor. 15:32) have some similarities with the Epicurean Philosophy: "Let us eat, drink and be merry for tomorrow we die!" However, Epicurus leaves out a few ingredients that the Bible adds to the formula: the ability to enjoy our

work and to see it as sacred (1 Tim. 4:4-5); and, secondly, the accumulation of spiritual treasures in the afterlife (Luke 12:19-21). Solomon says, "I have seen that it is from the hand of God" and this is why he says, "Tell yourself that your labor is good?" The enjoyment comes from the fact that *it is a reward from the hand of God for good.* Note carefully, he is not talking about salvation here but the enjoyment of this life "under the sun." The questions then are: What is the good of our labor? What makes it good or bad?

"For who can eat and who can have enjoyment without Him? For to a person who is good in His sight He has given wisdom and knowledge and joy, while to the sinner He has given the task of gathering and collecting so that he may give to one who is good in God's sight This too is vanity and striving after wind" (Eccl. 2:25-26). In all of this, God is still sovereign; and, thus, He is the great equalizer. We really are just passing through. I often remember how things were such a big deal to me in high school. It was of the utmost importance to get a letter jacket, to have the right car, and to have a date to the prom. Now, in retrospect, I wonder why in the world was I so preoccupied with those issues? They are all so irrelevant now. I can barely even remember the names of those with whom I graduated. If anything, I wish I would've studied harder and enjoyed more the simplicities of high school life. In many ways, like high school, we are only passing through. Life really is vaporous.

In similar fashion, why do I worry about the issues of life that do not make sense or fret that the blessings of life may fall on the wrong people? Life is a gift from God to be enjoyed by all and yet, the enjoyment of it comes only as we see it as a reward from his hand. Solomon closes this first section with, "This too is vanity and striving after wind." Life doesn't always make sense and, at times, there doesn't seem to be a plan; but there is, and He's unfolding it for you.

Good to Great, by Jim Collins is a best-selling secular book that analyzes how good companies become great companies. In the closing paragraph, he makes the following assessment: "When all the pieces come together, not only does your work move toward greatness, but so does your life. For in the end, it is impossible to have a great life unless it is a meaningful life. And it is very difficult to have a meaningful life without meaningful work. Perhaps, then, you might gain that rare tranquility that comes from knowing that you've had a hand in creating something of intrinsic excellence that makes a contribution. Indeed, you might even gain the deepest of all satisfactions: knowing that your short time here on earth has been well spent and that it mattered."[3]

These words in Collins's business book are, in many cases, better articulated than several commentaries on Ecclesiastes that I researched. As a student of church growth and missions, I have had the pleasure of meeting hundreds of believers over the years that are making a difference through a God-centered life and God-centered work. You will never hear or read about most of them, but the impact they are making is both eternal and significant. These people genuinely want to make a difference; they want to *carpe diem* because they have a deep understanding of God and His purpose for life. They aren't waiting to figure it all out before they accomplish something of significance.

CHAPTER 6

There Is a Plan
Ecclesiastes 3:1-15

—w—

Is it possible to make sense out of all the things that have happened in my life and to really believe that, in some supernatural way, it all intentionally fits into some kind of a plan? And if there is some plan for my life, do I have any say in it or am I sentenced to some fatalistic and predetermined course? If we have no influence or input, why bother? Watching our lives unfold can be frightening if we don't know how it's going to end. Is my life moving toward something good or something bad? What if I don't like the bag that was packed for me?

Jeremiah provides us with some positive news. He says, "For I know the plans I have for you,' declares the Lord, 'plans to prosper you and not to harm you, plans to give you hope and a future" (Jer. 29:11). Sometimes things seem senseless and meaningless. It would be incredible to believe that there was a wonderful and purposeful plan for my life. "Many are the plans in the mind of a man, but it is the purpose of the Lord that will stand" (Prov. 19:21).

Chapter three begins a new section. Solomon began with explaining to us that life is a gift from God which is given to enjoy. Kohelet is now going to provide insight into understanding the plan God is unfolding in our lives while on this earth. The plan is summarized in the first verse.

The Plan Summarized, 3:1

"There is an appointed time for everything. And there is a time for every event under heaven" (Eccl. 3:1). Here's the literal rendering, "To all a set time and a time for every purpose under the heavens." The *Message* says, "There's an opportune time to do things, a right time for everything on the earth." There is a concept called the "Providence of God." This is a reference to the providential care of God in each of our lives.

There is a "time." The Hebrew word *zeman* can also be translated "a season," but generally refers to specific points in time when events happen in your life. He says there is a "purpose," a delight, a pleasure, a good reason behind anything and everything that comes into your life. Psalm 37:23 says, "The steps of a man are established by the Lord; and he delights in his way." Now Solomon illustrates the point with a poem. This particular poem is considered to be one of the finest pieces of literature ever written and is often studied in college literature classes. One Hebrew scholar calls the poem the heart of the book of Ecclesiastes.

The Plan Illustrated, 3:2-8

In these verses you can see a list of pairs parallel to each other. The list consists of seven verses celebrating the doubling of the number seven. This is characteristic of Hebrew poetry. For ancient Hebrew poets, seven was the number of completion. Likewise, to double it was to intensify its meaning (example, Lord of lords, Kings of kings). This was intended to be a representative list of all aspects of living. The point is, there are no "oops" in your life. These kinds of things are simply the "times of your life." The poem begins with life and death, both of which lie beyond human control.

"A time to give birth and a time to die; a time to plant and a time to uproot what is planted. A time to kill and a time to heal; a time to tear down and a time to build up" (Eccl. 3:2-3).

"A time to kill..." This is one of the more controversial verses in the entire Bible. One of the *Ten Commandments* is, "Thou shalt not kill" (Exod. 20:13, *KJV*), and this appears to be an apparent contradiction.[1] However, Exodus 20:13 is better translated as, "You shall not murder." Simply put, there is never a time to take another person's life for self-serving or vengeful purposes. So what does it mean when he says there is "a time to kill"? Solomon is saying that there *is* a time to put to death.[2]

Then there are those times "to heal." We help those who are sick and do what we can to relieve their suffering. "There is a time to tear down and a time to build up," refers to the time required in building those stone structures and then tearing them down, replacing them with new structures. There are those times when we have to move over and give room for new things that need to come into being. I recently stepped aside after being senior pastor for twenty-fives years at the same church; but it was time for a younger man to come and lead this work where the Lord is taking it. We must always avoid freeze-framing certain eras or methodologies (the seven last words of the church: "We've never done it that way before").

"A time to weep and a time to laugh; a time to mourn and a time to dance" (Eccl. 3:4).

In his letter to the church in Rome, Paul says, "Rejoice with those who rejoice and weep with those who weep" (Rom. 12:15). Tears are part of life, but laughing is as well. A joyful heart is good medicine (Prov. 17:22), "but a crushed spirit dries up the bones."

"A time to throw stones and a time to gather stones" *(Eccl. 3:5a).* "What is throwing stones?" You're probably wondering how that can possibly be biblical. There are several views on this:

- First, in times of war, rocks were thrown on fields to render them useless if taken over by the enemy. Then in peacetime, rocks were gathered and arranged in terraces to hold the rain and prevent erosion.
- Secondly, shepherds kept stones in pouches to represent the number of sheep in their care. At times, the herd would increase, and at other times it would decrease. Thus, there were times of greater responsibility and times of lesser responsibility.
- Thirdly, merchants used stones to record commercial transactions—business will sometimes be up and sometimes be down.

"A time to embrace and a time to shun embracing" *(Eccl. 3:5b).* Some believe this refers to sexual relationships between a man and his wife. There are times to show affection and times not to show affection. Things are not always well, and peace at all costs is not always wise. There are those times when it must be known that there are problems and affection is absent until reconciliation has taken place.

"A time to search and a time to give up as lost; a time to keep and a time to throw away" *(Eccl. 3:6).* There are those times when the hard decisions of life must be made—decisions like when to stop looking for something and when to accept the fact that it is time to cut your losses and/or acknowledge that some things are gone for good.

"A time to tear apart and a time to sew together" *(Eccl. 3:7a).* Typically, this is understood as a reference to showing grief over the death of a loved one in which the bereaved would tear their garments as an expression of grief. The sewing of

those garments signaled the end of the mourning and getting on with life. However, the reference may also mean the everyday damage we inflict on ourselves, ripping our clothing and then fixing the damage and getting on with it.

"There is a time to be silent and a time to speak" (Eccl. 3:7b). Rabbi Ben Sira distinguished between two types of silence: one who keeps silent because he has no answer; the other keeps silent because he knows when to speak. There are times you say something, and then there are those times when it's best that you say nothing.

"A time to love and a time to hate" (Eccl. 3:8a). A time to love is something you'd expect from the Bible but "a time to hate"? Have you ever hated something? Sure you have, but isn't that sin? Is it? "But we're not supposed to hate people." Who's talking about people? When young Abraham Lincoln first saw a human being sold on the slave blocks in New Orleans, he felt hatred rising in his heart. He resolved that if he ever had the chance to do something about it, he would. (Read Eph. 4:26-27.)

"A time for war and a time for peace" (Eccl. 3:8b). There will be times of war with all its pain and, unfortunately, you may need to be part of that war. Then there will be times of peace. Solomon is commenting that if you enjoy the blessings of the one (peace), you need to also be willing to take the responsibility of the other (war).

The point of the poem is that there are appointed times in your life for all of the above. Life is not one long single narrative that ends up either tragic or not; rather life is made up of many *seasons*. Wisdom is taking what you have learned from the one and bringing that wisdom to the next. Part of wisdom is recognizing when a new season is beginning and the old one is coming to an end. The wise one wants to know what "time" (season) it is. Ascertaining what time it is in your life will give you a more supernatural perspective.

The Plan Explained, 3:9-15

"What profit is there to the worker from that in which he toils? I have seen the task which God has given the sons of men with which to occupy themselves" (Eccl. 3:9-10). In verse 9, we see the same question that was presented in verse 3: What is the real profit from the labor? What is the *yitron*? The answer provided by Solomon in verse 10 is that God has given us a task to "occupy" ourselves. A better translation would be "to be humbled by." But humbled by what, and in what way? There are some things in life we only learn by pain. Any of the things mentioned in Solomon's poem may not appear beautiful in themselves, but when they are seen as parts of the whole work of God's plan, we understand that He "has made" all things to fit in their appointed time and place. This word "appropriate" is translated "beautiful" in the King James Version. The word is *yaphah* and means that there is nothing wrong with it! The plan is absolutely perfect!

"He has set eternity in their hearts" (Eccl. 3:11). The Hebrew word is *olam*, "time without end." What God does will be beautiful; but we want to see the whole (*olam*) now; yet we see only the part because we are *ha adam*, mortal men, under the sun, finite in our existence. If you dash into a theater and watch five minutes of a two-hour feature, you are not going to see the beauty of the theme. Humanity was created with an inborn inquisitiveness to learn how everything we experience can be integrated into a whole. The beauty of a plan is not in its parts but in its whole. That's why life will remain an enigma until men learn to fear God!

"I know that there is nothing better for them than to rejoice and to do good in one's lifetime; moreover, that every man who eats and drinks sees good in all his labor—it is the gift of God. I know that everything God does will remain forever; there is nothing to add to it and there is nothing to take from it, for God has so worked that men should fear Him" (Eccl. 3:12-14). Verses 12 and 13 are reflective of

the first two chapters reminding us that God is in control. Behind our free choices stands the will of God that orders events in our lives with a view to a plan for eternity. Our part in the plan is revealed here: "For God has so worked that men should fear him." The fear of God is a recurring theme in Ecclesiastes. (See 5:7; 7:18; 8:12-13; 12:13.) The fear is of *ha elohim.* Usually it is the fear of "Jehovah," God's personal covenant name with Israel. But here it is fear of the Creator, the maker of all.

This is the same "fear" described as the "beginning of knowledge" in Proverbs 1:7. Look at Exodus 20:18-21. The whole event was designed to instill fear. Why? In Exodus 20:20, the same word for fear is repeated as a pun. They were not to be terrified but to fear. God frightened them so they would remember who He is. They would also remember who they were not. God had taken the terror out of fear which leaves reverence! This is our part of the plan.

Another word in the New Testament that carries the same concept is "faith." This is what life is all about. You can have your questions, your confusion, your doubts, but never use them as a reason for not fearing your God. His understanding is infinite and ours is finite. What happens when you try to pour the infinite into the finite? It's called spillage and another word for that is *mystery.*

How do you respond to someone you fear? As Solomon says later, *"The conclusion, when all has been heard, is: fear God and keep His commandments" (Eccl. 12:13).* You keep His commandments, you obey what He instructs, whether you agree or not. It's obedience that produces the enjoyment of the plan. This is the "Whole of Man." This is what it means to be human. Judgment will determine just how human you were.

"That which is has been already and that which will be has already been, for God seeks what has passed by" (Eccl. 3:15). The plan of God will not change, it is established. It all

fits. He makes the past fit with the present and the present fit with the future. All the things in my past, my hurts and tears, my joys and victories, my failures and embarrassments, all fit to make me uniquely me, preparing me for my future according to the plan of God. There is a plan if we let God be God! "The secret things belong to the Lord our God, but the things revealed belong to us and to our children forever, that we may follow all the words of this law" (Deut. 29:29). Therefore, I don't have to be able to explain everything; but I do need to fear God and watch His plan for my life unfold before my eyes.

- "But the plans of the Lord stand firm forever, the purposes of his heart through all generations" (Ps. 33:11).
- "In his heart a man plans his course, but the Lord determines his steps" (Prov. 16:9).
- "I make known the end from the beginning, from ancient times, what is still to come. I say: My purpose will stand, and I will do all that I please" (Isa. 46:10).
- "And we know that in all things God works for the good of those who love him, who have been called according to his purpose" (Rom. 8:28).

CHAPTER 7

Life Isn't Fair
Ecclesiastes 3:16-22

—ɯ—

How often have you explained, perhaps to your children, that life is not always fair? And yet, there's something in us that still wants to believe that *it is* fair. Sad endings may make us cry, but we can handle that. Years ago Holly and I went to see *Romeo and Juliet* (talk about not fair!). As we were waiting for the first performance to file out, I noticed that there were women crying (and a lot of men struggling with their allergies), but some of them were mad; we hate it when the bad guys win. If Cinderella's cruel, ugly, stepsister had ended up with Prince Charming, we would have been mad! Remember what you learned as a child at the cafeteria? You *always* wait in line for your turn. How do you feel today when someone cuts into the line? Do you find yourself praying for patience? Or vengeance? Why? Because it's not fair! Injustice disturbs us because we still want to believe that life is fair. But is it?

In the previous chapter, we read how God has a plan for our lives. Everything that happens to us has an appointed time, and it all fits together into something that makes sense within the grand scheme of things. The problem with the plan is that we don't always know what "time" it is. In other words, we can't always (if ever) make sense of the "appointed times" for things that come into our lives. I like to refer to these seasons as the "why me, God?" times. Sometimes life doesn't seem to make sense. Worse, sometimes there seems to be no rhyme or reason for the events that unfold. However, not to sound harsh or insensitive, but that's our problem, not God's. Simply because particular events do not make sense to me (and my three-pound brain), it doesn't mean they don't make sense to the One who spoke galaxies into existence.

Here in the last part of Ecclesiastes 3, Kohelet talks about the objections that would seduce me into rejecting the whole idea that there is a plan for my life. The first two objections have to do with why there is injustice and why good people die. We know that the Bible says, "It's appointed for man once to die and after that, judgment" (Heb. 9:27). We know that God will judge the wicked someday at the proper time (Eccl. 12:14), but why someday? Why not now? What's the delay? Why isn't the present the proper time for universal justice? Why injustice? Why do bad things happen to good people?

The Presence of Injustice, 3:16-17

The Bible never denies that there is injustice in the world. As a matter of fact, Solomon tells us why God permits it: *"Furthermore, I have seen under the sun that in the place of justice there is wickedness and in the place of righteousness there is wickedness" (Eccl. 3:16).*

Again, he says he saw "under the sun in the place of justice, wickedness and in the place of righteousness, wickedness." *Resha* is the Hebrew word for "wickedness," a bending or perversion of what is right. The courtroom is the very place you would expect to find justice and yet, it can be the very place you find the perversion of it. We need to remember that the courts and government of our land will always be a reflection of its people. But, if this is the case, why would the Apostle Paul say what he does in Romans 13:1-4? "Every person is to be in subjection to the governing authorities, for there is no authority except from God, and those which exist are established by God. Therefore, whoever resists authority has opposed the ordinance of God; and they who have opposed will receive condemnation upon themselves. For rulers are not a cause of fear for good behavior, but for evil. Do you want to have no fear of authority? Do what is good and you will have praise from the same; for it is a minister of God to you for good. But if you do what is evil, be afraid; for it does not bear the sword for nothing; for it is a minister of God, an avenger who brings wrath on the one who practices evil." The answer is in Romans 13:5: "Therefore it is necessary to be in subjection, not only because of wrath, but also for conscience sake." Some things just do not make sense:

- In some states a girl must have the permission of her parents to have her ears pierced, but in those same states she can get an abortion without her parents ever knowing.
- Have you ever heard of Larry Singleton? He was convicted of the rape, battery and cutting off the arms of a fifteen-year-old girl. He's out of prison after eight years.
- In a ruling of the U.S. Circuit Court of Appeals, a conviction of a man accused of fatally injuring a fetus was upheld. The Ruling was as follows: "In view of…infants who died subsequent to birth due to fetal injuries as human beings, it seems clear that Congress intended fetal infanticide to be included within the definition of murder." The man is serving a fifteen-year prison sentence. However, if a doctor ends the life of a fetus, it's referred to as an abortion. Is something inconsistent here?

"I thought in my heart, 'God will bring to judgment both the righteous and the wicked, for there will be a time for every activity, a time for every deed'" (Eccl. 3:17, NIV). Once again, Solomon communes in his heart and asks himself the hard questions of what he saw to be true. Some call him a cynic. Others say he's being heretical. But asking the hard questions doesn't make you a cynic or a heretic. It simply makes you a person asking honest questions. God will judge both. Justice delayed is not justice denied. "The Lord is not slow in keeping his promise, as some understand slowness. He is patient with you, not wanting anyone to perish, but everyone to come to repentance" (2 Pet. 3:9, *NIV*). But why wait? What if His judgment fell upon you before you repented? Solomon says, "God will bring to judgment both the righteous and the wicked, for there will be a time for every activity, a time for every deed" (3:17, *NIV*). What does this mean?

It means that with God, there is a "time of judgment and retribution"; every act and every injustice shall be punished. But it is in *His* time. In John's vision of the end times, saints are still asking the same question, "They called out in a loud voice, 'How long, Sovereign Lord, holy and true, until you judge the inhabitants of the earth and avenge our blood'" (Rev. 20:11-15). The world is not a fair place, yet God will judge it at the appointed time. But why isn't today the appointed time?

The Testing of Injustice, 3:18-22

"I said to myself concerning the sons of men, 'God has surely tested them in order for them to see that they are but beasts'" (Eccl. 3:18). Solomon communes in his heart and reflects on the "sons of men," (*beni ha adam*) the "sons of Adam," our human race. "God has surely tested them." God has allowed injustice for a purpose, a good reason, and that good reason is to expose something about us as human beings.

God is testing us to show that we are "beasts" (*hem behemah*). We die like cattle, and we are not qualified to be a god!

The temptation to be a god is one of the oldest temptations in the book. As early as Genesis 3:5, we see a part of Satan's temptation to humanity included the statement: "You will be like God." Man was never designed to be the center of his own universe. He is not capable of assuming the role of determining right and wrong, just and unjust. Injustice exists because man rules as a god and man doesn't make for a just god.

In the Darwinian worldview, man is the apex of the evolutionary process. He is answerable to no one, especially God, because he thinks himself to be a god. Injustice exists because it comes from the heart of man and man is not a just "god." Man has degraded himself to the point where he can no longer understand his own degradation (Rom. 1:28-32). We are like "beasts" (Eccl. 3:18) because we are not the self-sufficient, just masters of the universe. We do not make for good gods. This is evident by the fact that we are surrounded with injustice. God is not to blame—man is; we are like beasts because we have no understanding of justice. Furthermore, we are like cattle because we are as frail as all other creatures. You find the same two observations in Psalm 49:12, 20. Man is "without understanding" and "will not endure." That does not make for such a great god!

"For the fate of the sons of men and the fate of beasts is the same. As one dies so dies the other; indeed, they all have the same breath and there is no advantage for man over beast, for all is vanity. All go to the same place. All came from the dust and all return to the dust" (Eccl. 3:19-20). With cattle and all other creatures, we share the "same breath"; and thus, we have no superiority over animals when it comes to the breath of life (Ps. 104:24-30). When it comes to suffering and dying, there is no difference between humanity and the animals. This also is *hevel*, for it does not make sense to us

in this passing life, but it is the way it is. We all experience death. A dying Napoleon Bonaparte summed it up in these words: "I die before my time; and my body will be given back to the earth, to become the food of worms. Such is the fate which so soon awaits the Great Napoleon."

All men and cattle are buried, and the earth serves as a universal tomb for all creatures. It is from "dust to dust" for all.

"Who knows that the breath of man ascends upward and the breath of the beast descends downward to the earth?" (Eccl. 3:21). Is this a question or is it a statement of fact? It begins with *mi yodhea*, "who knows?" The verbs "to go upward" and "to go downward" are actually participles with an article attached to them. In other words he is saying, "Who knows the breath of life of man; is it the one going upward or is the breath of life of the beast the one going downward?" Solomon has already said in 3:17 that men will stand before God. There is no question in his mind. He says the same thing in 12:7. The fact that the "breath of life" (the life of a man) goes to God is stated in the oldest book of the Bible: "Even after my skin is destroyed, yet from my flesh I shall see God" (Job 19:26). Psalm 49:14-15 says, "Like sheep they are destined for the grave and death will feed on them. The upright will rule over them in the morning; their forms will decay in the grave, far from their princely mansions. But God will redeem my life from the grave; he will surely take me to himself." Humanity and animals are alike in that we experience the frailty of life and ultimately death. While we all return to dust, the difference is that at death the human soul returns to his maker.

"I have seen that nothing is better than that man should be happy in his activities, for that is his lot, for who will bring him to see what will occur after him?" (Eccl. 3:22). Or, as Jesus said, "Therefore do not worry about tomorrow, for tomorrow will worry about itself. Each day has enough trouble of its own" (Matt. 6:34).

We are unable to know the future and, thus, it is important for us to enjoy life and grab the moments of each day. Enjoy what you *do* know and trust God with what you don't. Simply put, get the most enjoyment out of each day and leave to God that which you cannot understand. This is illustrated for us in the book of Job. God never really answers Job's question regarding, "why me God?" However, God does say to Job, "Can you bind the chains of the Pleiades, or loose the cords of Orion? Can you lead forth a constellation in its season, and guide the Bear [Big Dipper] with her cubs?" (Job 38:31-32). Job could not. But, God can. We admit that God has infinite wisdom; why would we expect to fully comprehend infinite wisdom with only our finite capacity? We may not understand everything, but what we can comprehend is the fact that God is in control, and He has our best interests at heart. Thus, we apprehend that which we cannot totally comprehend.

The key to "the plan" is apprehending and resting in the fact that God is God and that we are not. We are reminded of this by the fact that we, like the animal kingdom, also have a mortal lifespan and without God, we are devoid of moral justice. It is God who sets the moral boundaries. Devoid of Him, our mortality and justice are completely dependant upon man. Human history has demonstrated our failure in this. Without God's guidance, we are limited to our own perspectives on morality. As long as man tries to rule as a god on this earth, we will continue to experience injustice and death because—I'll say it again—man does not make for a good god. The problem, of course, is that none of us is qualified to be a god. In fact, because we are corrupt (Rom. 3:10), we are unjust and can compound the problem when we attempt to rule our world. This is the source of injustice! Solomon is very specific in pointing out that humanity is the source of injustice. Nevertheless, humanity still strives to live as if we can rule this world.

Take comfort in the fact that you are *not* a god. He knows what's best and has it figured out. We must apprehend this truth even if we are unable to comprehend it. What's keeping you from enjoying the "Plan"? Who would you rather have in control? Who is better qualified to rule your life?

CHAPTER 8

Success Can Be Lethal
Ecclesiastes 4:1-8

—ᘜ—

After watching several episodes of the TV reality show, *VH1 Goes Inside*, I noticed a pattern. The series typically provides an overview into how various musical groups became successful. First, I noticed that often these groups would arise out of very non-promising beginnings. Second, they would experience success through a "big break" or through perseverance; then the pressures of pride and fame would often become the demise of the group, resulting in their breakup. For some, the demise would include the need for rehabilitation as a result of drug or alcohol abuse. For others, it would result in divorce or bitterness. A few groups would strive to find fame again through a reunion.

Success is not a bad word. God has not called us to be "failures." Nevertheless, like all good things, there needs to be a warning because even success can be hazardous to your health. In Ecclesiastes 4:1-8, Solomon shows how success can affect people in three different ways:

1. First, there's the person who just can't get "it" (success) going because he's oppressed by the successful.

2. Second, there's the individual who finally gets "it" going at great personal cost to himself.
3. Finally, there's the guy who has "it" going but it's not enough because he never answers the ultimate question.

Those Who Are Oppressed, 4:1-3

"Then I looked again at all the acts of oppression which were being done under the sun and behold I saw the tears of the oppressed and that they had no one to comfort them; and on the side of their oppressors was power, but they had no one to comfort them" (Eccl. 4:1).

"Oppression" is the miscarriage of justice. It is another "not fair" in this world of ours; and it doesn't come from God but from us. Oppression is injustice authored by selfishness. Whether intentional or not, oppression is the hindrance to the success and/or wellbeing of others because of careless and selfish disregard for another's well being. The "oppressors" are the ones with the "power." What power? Like success, power is not necessarily a bad thing, but it is mishandled when it is not used to benefit others. The Hebrew word translated "power" means strength for the ability to do good. What good? The implementation of the power to aid in the welfare of others. The oppressed are often limited in the ability to express themselves except through tears. God did not design us to enjoy that experience. Thus, the tears! The "ragged-edge" reality of it all is that this is happening "under the sun" *where man is in charge*; the self proclaimed and selfish "god," who rules and oppresses his own. The motto of this worldview is: "I have mine and you can't have it. You have yours and I want it!"

"So I congratulated the dead who are already dead more than the living who are still living" (Eccl. 4:2). What is this? Realism! Let's face it; they would be better off dead! At least the dead have escaped the miseries of such oppression.

Because the dead have escaped the oppression of this world, Solomon's logic says: *"But better off than both of them is the one who has never existed, who has never seen the evil activity that is done under the sun" (Eccl. 4:3).*

Better? Solomon says they are better off compared to those who had to suffer under this "evil activity" (*ha rah*: the evil). *Rah* means misery and injury to another; and in this context, the "injury" is in not relieving some of the suffering. Therefore, Solomon congratulates them.

Those Who Are Competitive, 4:4-6

"I have seen that every labor and every skill which is done is the result of rivalry between a man and his neighbor. This too is vanity and striving after wind" (Eccl. 4:4). You have probably heard that you must be aggressive and ruthless in this world if you're going to get ahead. There is no denying that there is some truth to that thinking. Failure to "look out for number one" may result in your ambitions and welfare being oppressed. Not many "under the sun" are going to devote much time and energy to your welfare, success, and happiness. By the way, praise God for the few exceptions—they are called friends (Prov. 18:24). Most do not have many friends, and many do not have any. We would like to believe that we work hard for good motives like love of family, concern for the community, and service to God. But Solomon says, for the most part, we are fooling ourselves. The truth is, most work is done because of "rivalry between a man and his neighbor."

How often is success defined in terms of being better than the guy next to you? How much injustice do you believe is produced by envy? We use the phrase "healthy competition." When it brings the best out by stretching us a little, then indeed it's healthy; but it becomes unhealthy when the goal is only to be "better than." When this is the real objective, beware of the temptation to cheat and/or develop resentment at the accomplishments of others. Furthermore, resist the opportunity to undermine their success by risking your own integrity.

Alexis De Tocqueville, a French writer and politician of the nineteenth century, said this of America: "I sought for the greatness and genius of America in her commodious harbors and her ample rivers, and it was not there; in the fertile fields and the boundless prairies, and it was not there; not until I went into the churches of America and heard her pulpits aflame with righteousness did I understand the secrets of her genius and power. America is great because she is good, and if America ever ceases to be good, America will cease to be great!"

The cancer of greatness for a man or woman is the oppressive mentality to be more successful than someone else. This word "rivalry" is the same translated often as "jealousy." Delitzsch, in his commentary, puts it this way: "All the expenditure of strength and art has covetousness and envy, with which one seeks to surpass another, as its poisoned sting."[1]

It's not so much that we want to have things but that we want to be admired for the things we have. This desire to be admired is the spark of most competitiveness. Isn't it amazing what people will do to get attention? Solomon says this competitiveness is vaporous and passes too quickly to make any good sense of it. Therefore, perhaps the wiser thing to do is to forget this type of competitiveness and drop out of the "rat race." Solomon knew we would be thinking this, so he checks us with a Proverb.

"The fool folds his hands and consumes his own flesh" *(Eccl. 4:5).* In the 1960's, a lot of Americans learned this for themselves in the Hippie movement and at Woodstock. As they dropped out of society and moved into a "counter-culture" movement, they found themselves devouring themselves, their health, their resources, and their self-respect (Prov. 6:10).

The lazy will not be successful in anything, not even in his ideals, but rather his laziness will destroy him. God has designed us to feel good about our labor (Eccl. 2:24). There is no spiritual premium for laziness. In his second letter to the church at Thessalonica, a city influenced by various trendy Greek philosophies, Paul taught that people shouldn't eat unless they worked (2 Thess. 3:10). Kohelet follows this proverb with another proverb that puts the whole thing in perspective.

"One hand full of rest is better than two fists full of labor and striving after wind" (Eccl. 4:6). In this verse, the first reference to the word "hands" is descriptive of a hand that is open, ready to receive and to give back. The second, "fists," refers to two hands cupped together to get all they can. He is saying it is better to have less and enjoy it with rest than to have more and be struggling for it. (See also Prov. 15:16-17; 16:8; 17:1; Phil. 4:11-13.) If this doesn't happen, we have a real problem on our hands (pun intended) for we will become…

Those Who Are Compulsive, 4:7-8

"Then I looked again at vanity under the sun. There was a certain man without a dependent, having neither a son nor a brother, yet there was no end to all his labor. Indeed, his eyes were not satisfied with riches and he never asked, 'And for whom am I laboring and depriving myself of pleasure? This too is vanity and it is a grievous task'" (Eccl. 4:7-8).

There is a man, a solitary man, who has no one else depending on him; no wife, no children, no relatives, absolutely no one to share what he has and yet, there is no end to his labor. He is a driven man, gratified only by accomplishments and preoccupied with symbols of success. He is highly competitive and abnormally busy. For some it's because they are still trying to prove to their fathers they aren't "bums." For others, perhaps there were not enough "well-dones" passed out when they were young. Regardless, the common denominator for both is that they live to please *man*, not God. Where does it all take you? In December 1976, *Time Magazine* featured an article about a man who had accumulated 2.3 billion dollars before he died. The article made this observation: "He emerges from the hidden years as a tortured, troubled man, who wallowed in self-neglect, lapsed into periods of near-lunacy, lived without comfort or joy in prison-like conditions, and ultimately died for lack of a medical device that his own foundation had helped to develop." Such was the end of life for Howard Hughes. "Success" claimed another victim.[2]

When do we ask ourselves "The Question?" *Why am I doing this?* The "compulsive" can't answer that question with anything that makes sense. What is exposed is the drive to achieve and to acquire. One commentator says, "It nudges us from bed early and keeps us in the factory or office late. Long after we have enough to care for our own needs, some of us keep pushing for more." (How big of a pile do you really want to be sitting on when Jesus returns?)

What is the answer to the question, "Why am I doing this?" The goods God has given were never intended to make the rich richer, but to serve the needs of all God's people. The drive to accumulate goods must be accompanied by an urge to share them. If not, then injustice is the result (1 Tim. 6:6). People with ingenuity, energy, and opportunity can hoard huge resources while others go begging. The goodness of enjoyment is in the sharing of those goods with others (2 Cor. 9:10-14).

Leslie Brandt said: "As for me, my heart waits on God. I know that my salvation comes from him. I may change my views about many things; but as for my need for God and his love, that is one conviction which shall never change.

"There are many who would like to sabotage a man's deepest convictions. With the skillful use of words and logic they try to destroy the very foundations of his faith. As for me, my heart waits on God.

"He is my hope and my help. The temporal values that men focus on is so quickly lost amidst the tempests of this life. Their highest aspirations burst forth like bright flares only to fizzle out like wet fuses. But God offers a security that is eternal. It is not logically defined, but it is experienced."[3]

Are you telling yourself the truth about success? How is it affecting your life? Here's your homework:

1. Are you *"The Oppressed"*? If yes, where is your hope? Is it in God or in man? What does that mean to you? Stop being a victim.
2. Are you *"The Competitive"*? Then what is success to you? How will you know when you have it?
3. Are you *"The Compulsive"*? Then ask the question, why are you doing it all?

CHAPTER 9

Life Is More Than Coping
Ecclesiastes 4:9-16

—ɯ—

In his book, *You Gotta Keep Dancing*, Tim Hansel says, "The most important thing to keep remembering is that life is not so much meant to be understood as it is to be lived out; it is not a problem to be solved, but a mystery to be participated in fully. Let yourself be surprised."[1]

Sometimes we get so busy coping with life that we actually begin to believe that life is primarily focused on mostly survival from crisis to crisis. However, Solomon says that God has a plan for each of us and yet...*why do things have to be so difficult?* Solomon directs our attention to this objection.

How could there be a good plan when there seems to be so much trouble? First, we must take into account the source of the trouble. Mankind is the source of life's injustices. Mankind is the one who fancies himself to be a god and rules this world with his own divinity, and it is from his throne we see pain and oppression. As long as man rules this earth, there will always be injustice and yet, God still has a plan. Even with the injustices of men, He will still bring about his will for you and me (Rom. 8:28).

Life is the adventure of being surprised and watching his plan unfold. If you've convinced yourself life is merely coping with crisis, you'll miss the whole objective of living. In chapter 4:9-16, Kohelet is going to give us some helpful advice on how to actually see God's plan for your own life unfold. *But* you're going to need a little help from your friends. We tend to be isolated people. Generally, there seems to be a low degree of involvement in each other's lives. Privacy seems to be such a cherished prize for some reason and yet, what does it produce? There is a gradual movement as we grow toward isolation. Indirectly, we are proclaiming independence from each other and from God.

D. Vance Packer described the United States as "The Nation of Strangers." He illustrated this with the fact that protecting our privacy has become *en vogue*. For example, in the nineteenth and early twentieth centuries, American homes were built with porches in *front* of our houses. They were later moved to the back of the homes; and now in the twenty-first century homes are often built with walls in our backyard in order that no one can disturb our privacy. Technological advancements have made it easier for us to become more private and less social (e.g. video games, ATMs, internet dating, etc.). When I speak to our emerging generation, I find that commitment to a relationship is somewhat of an old fashioned concept.

There is, however, a down side to relationships. There is a cost involved, and they require work and sacrifice. Friendships require that we sacrifice independence. The *cost* is consulting another's feelings on things, listening to another's point of view, adjusting to another's lifestyle, and keeping faith with another's trust. Is it really worth it? Solomon believes it is. The power of friendships and the power of experience are crucial, and you need them both to live out God's plan for your life.

The Power of Friendships, 4:9-12

"Two are better than one because they have a good return for their labor" (Eccl. 4:9).

He begins with the foundational truth that it is better not to be alone. This is a direct blow against isolation and reclusive behavior. From the beginning, we were created to be in relationship with God *and* with one another. Genesis says, "The Lord God said, 'It is not good for the man to be alone'" (Gen. 2:18). Although this focused on marriage, it is not limited to it for the context is partnership, companionship between people. Proverbs 18:24 says, "A man of many companions may come to ruin, but there is a friend who sticks closer than a brother." The common word for a friend is *reah* and is usually translated as "neighbor." It can refer to most of our relationships from the guy who is suing you (18:17) to the one loving you at all times (17:17).

But the second word is *aheb* and means the "one who loves." Solomon has much to say in Proverbs about *this* friend:

1. He will be committed to you. He'll be there (18:24; 27:10).
2. He will be honest with you (27:6, 17).
3. He will have counsel for you (27:9).
4. He will protect your feelings (25:17, 20; 26:18-19; 27:14).

When you are this kind of friend (and have this kind of a friend) you enjoy three blessings from God in that friendship. These blessings will cause you to see His plan *for your life* unfold.

They provide assistance in time of failure, 4:10: *"For if either of them falls, the one will lift up his companion. But woe to the one who falls when there is not another to lift him up" (Eccl. 4:10).* He illustrates the first advantage of companionship with one traveling alone in rough terrain who slips and falls, possibly into a pit or crevice. Ordinarily, he would risk the possibility of death from exposure or injury, *but* there's another to pick him up. In times of failure, we need someone. Fleeing for his life from King Saul, David (Solomon's father), "escaped to the cave of Adullam; and when his brothers and all of his father's household heard of it, they went down there to him" (1 Sam. 22:1).

They provide comfort in times of need, 4:11: *"Furthermore, if two lie down together they keep warm, but how can one be warm alone?" (Eccl. 4:11).* Winter nights in Israel are cold. The outer garment you wore during the day was your only covering at night. The mutual warmth shared when two would lie close to each other provided what one alone could not. This may sound romantic, but that's not the point here (see Song of Solomon for that). Here, he's referring to comfort and warmth when it's cold and to genuine encouragement when there is discouragement. Many of us have been prepared, even by the injustices of man, to give comfort to others.

They provide defense in time of danger, 4:12: *"And if one can overpower him who is alone, two can resist him. A cord of three strands is not quickly torn apart" (Eccl. 4:12).* This third example also involves a traveler. Like today, ancient travelers experienced the threat of bandits. To have someone with you decreased your odds of being attacked but, by contrast, we become an easier target when we travel alone.

He adds to this another proverb, "A cord of three strands is not quickly torn apart." The cord of three strands was the strongest cord made at that time. The number three was a symbol of strength and completeness for it was a number that could not be divided easily. If the companionship of two is better than one, then the addition of another is even better. The sum of the whole is greater than its parts. From this comes great strength against attack. This is why marriage is based upon covenants made to a third person—Jesus Christ (Eph. 5).

The first way you're going to see God's plan unfold before your eyes will be through your friends as they assist, comfort and protect you. The second is through...

The Value of Accepting Instruction, 4:13

"A poor yet wise lad is better than an old and foolish king who no longer knows how to receive instruction" (Eccl. 4:13). The key to living a wise life is to "know how to receive instruction," literally, "warnings" (Prov. 1:1-7; 3:1-8). The protection is in the counsel of others who have gone before us in life. (See also Prov. 11:14; 15:22; 24:5-6; 26:12.) *Yellow Flag*: Sometimes age and position only fossilizes one's self-will because there's more prestige to protect. The proof that wisdom does not necessarily come with age and position is that...

We learn that admiration fades, 4:14-16: *"For he has come out of prison to become king, even though he was born poor in his kingdom. I have seen all the living under the sun throng to the side of the second lad who replaces him. There is no end to all the people, to all who were before them, and even the ones who will come later will not be happy with him, for this too is vanity and striving after wind" (Eccl. 4:14-16).*

Initially, this is a little confusing. Who is "he"? Is this the new wise "lad" who is going to replace him and then be replaced by another after him? Either way, the point of the illustration is that no matter how you arrived at success, remember how you got there. Whether it was the rough road out of poverty and prison or given to you on a silver platter like Solomon, fame fades quickly. Age and position are the last excuses we have for not growing or changing. As we grow older, we are in danger of losing our teachable spirits.

The reason it's difficult to remain teachable is because it is so hard to admit when we're wrong!

Who do you have in your life that functions as your counselors? Seek their counsel for the Lord's counsel for every major decision that affects your life. In a fire, the hottest ember will still cool and die if removed from the rest of the embers. Who are your embers? Pray and ask for God to send you more.

CHAPTER 10

Wisdom in Worship
Ecclesiastes 5:1-7

—〰—

Have you ever arrived at church on a Sunday and, after scurrying around to find a parking spot and then room on the pew for you and your family, you sat there wondering, "What am I doing here anyway?" We come to what we call a "worship service" in a "worship center" with "worship music" and with "worshipful attitudes" to "worship God" yet, none of us had "Worship 101" in school. What are we supposed to do? What is a "worshipful attitude" anyway? What is worship?

In *Worship: Rediscovering the Missing Jewel*, Dr. Ron Allen says, "Worship is an active response to God whereby we declare His worth." William Temple, the Archbishop of Canterbury from 1942 to 1945, said, "to worship is to quicken the conscience by the holiness of God, to feed the mind with the truth of God, to purge the imagination by the beauty of God, to open the heart to the love of God, and to open the will to the purpose of God."

In writing *Ecclesiastes*, Solomon is not trying to be cynical, nor is he bitter as some claim; rather he is asking real questions about real life. He has been talking to us about the plan God has for each of us and how that plan unfolds. It was just a matter of time before he would get to this question about worshiping the God who has the plan.

The most intimate and personal thing in life is how we worship God. Everyone worships! If it's not God then it's some*one* or some*thing* else. You can learn a lot about a person by knowing what it is they worship and how they worship. We reflect who or what it is we honor.

Who or what do we look up to? We tend to imitate our heroes. For those who do worship God, how do we do it? Perhaps a better question is how *should* we worship?

Solomon provides us with some insight into how we can worship God "in spirit and truth" (John 4:24). In Ecclesiastes 5, he begins with what should be on our minds when we enter a place for worship, i.e. don't be in any hurry to do anything, but *be quick*. The wisdom writing of James in the New Testament gives us a clue how to approach God in worship: "But let everyone be quick to hear, slow to speak and slow to anger" (Jas. 1:19).

Be Quick to Listen! 5:1

"Guard your steps as you go to the house of God and draw near to listen rather than to offer the sacrifice of fools; for they do not know they are doing evil" (Eccl. 5:1). When you come into the "House of God" guard your steps. Be aware of what it is you are about to do and why you are going to do it. At the time of Solomon, the "House of God" was actually the Temple that God had commissioned him to build (1 Kings 6:1).

After chasing the vendors away from the Temple outer court, Jesus said "Is it not written, 'My house will be called a house of prayer for all nations?' But you have made it a 'robbers' den'" (Mark 11:17). Some readers are initially disturbed that Jesus would actually make a scene by over-turning the tables of the vendors. This couldn't have been good for public relations, and I'm guessing that it was also probably politically incorrect. For various reasons, people think of Jesus as a very stoic emotionless type (like Dr. Spock on *Star Trek*), whereas others seem to envision him as having the personality of Mr. Rogers. Here, however, we see God's indignation over the lack of reverence that had infiltrated the Temple. Simply put, we see that God takes this subject of worship very seriously. The purpose of the Temple was worship. Most local assemblies of believers (the Church) construct buildings for the practical purpose of having a place to corporately worship, to disciple, for spiritual enrichment, etc. Most of these assemblies have what's known as a worship center or sanctuary.

What images come to mind when you think of worship? Typically we think of singing, praising, music, thanksgiving, and prayer. Each of these elements is indeed a part of worship, but Solomon says that the prerequisite is to come with the intent to *listen!* In Hebrew this word carries the connotation that "we draw near to hear!" Thus, we go to the house of the Lord to listen, not to tell God what He should be doing. There are times in our worship that we talk too much and listen very little.

Listen? There is a double force to the Hebrew word, which is usually lost when translated into English. Within the context of Ecclesiastes, listening meant to pay attention for the purpose of obeying. Jesus comments on this in Luke 8:18, "Therefore consider carefully how you listen. Whoever has will be given more; whoever does not have, even what he thinks he has will be taken from him" (*NIV*). The alternative is to offer up the "sacrifice of fools" (Eccl. 5:1) which is empty worship or rituals without meaning.

The purpose of an "offering" was to bring one into communion with God by removing anything that interfered with that communion. The offering brought forgiveness because it was accompanied by a contrite heart expressing thanksgiving. The "sacrifice of fools" on the other hand was an offering that was treated like magic. They incorrectly believed that the offering was like an incantation, a formula to manipulate spiritual powers. Whenever ritual replaces purpose, the reality is that we are no longer worshipping.

Magic is the manipulation of spiritual powers in order to serve your own best interests! Within Christianity we may see this in various ways: pray this prayer seven times, forward the email and God will bless you, send a particular ministry $100 and God will bless you ten-fold, or go to church each Sunday and God will bless you at work. If everything works according to such 'law,' then God is no longer sovereign and there is no place for grace. The power of believing becomes a form of magic attempting to manipulate spiritual forces for you own longings. Are we talking about faith or sorcery?

Magic is not worship and is obviously contrary to biblical worship. Worship begins with your mouths closed and ears opened to listen with the anticipation of obeying. Samuel asked, "Has the Lord as much delight in burnt offerings and sacrifices as in obeying the voice of the Lord? Behold, to obey is better than sacrifice, and to heed than the fat of rams" (1 Sam. 15:22).

In Psalm 51:16-17, David says: "You do not delight in sacrifice, or I would bring it; you do not take pleasure in burnt offerings. The sacrifices of God are a broken spirit; a broken and a contrite heart, O God, you will not despise." Solomon adds in Proverbs 15:8: "The Lord detests the sacrifice of the wicked, but the prayer of the upright pleases him" (*NIV*).

Unknowingly, our attempt to worship God may actually be irreverent in His sight. We need to be wise and know exactly what we are doing when we worship. We must come prepared to listen to whatever it is God has to say to us and respond in obedience. And this is why we will ...

Be Slow to Speak, 5:2-3

"Do not be hasty in word or impulsive in thought to bring up a matter in the presence of God. For God is in heaven and you are on the earth; therefore let your words be few" (Eccl. 5:2). Before we come to him asking for things, Solomon says, "Don't be hasty in word," nor "impulsive in thought." The Hebrew rendering is "don't rush to open your mouth nor hurry your heart." Before you speak, think! What is it you really desire to bring before God? "God is in heaven and you are on the earth" That doesn't mean that God is millions of miles away (Psalm 139:1-6). What it does mean is that you are not His peer, and He doesn't work for you!

Solomon says that when we go into His presence, "Let your words be few." Jesus warned of many words in Matthew 6:7, "And when you pray, do not keep on babbling like pagans, for they think they will be heard because of their many words" (*NIV*). This became a Talmudic precept—to let the words of a man always be few in the presence of God, according to what was written." Do we prepare what we really want to present to God? How do we express it? What is the one thing you are most concerned about? How can we listen for the answer if we don't know our deep desires?

We do have communion with our Heavenly Father as a child with a loving parent; yet we need to remember that He is still the parent. (See Rom. 8:14-15; Heb. 4:15-16.)

Solomon gives us another proverb to reiterate the point. *"For the dream comes through much effort, and the voice of a fool through many words" (Eccl. 5:3).*

Just as dreams can result from much stress, so a multitude of words from a fool create the same. Solomon's point here is that when we come to worship, we come not to talk but first to let God talk, and then we listen. When we speak, it should only be after we have given contemplative thought to what we want to say to the Creator of the stars. After God has spoken and after we have listened, we may want to continue in our worship. "Ascribe to the Lord, O sons of the mighty, ascribe to the Lord glory and strength. Ascribe to the Lord the glory due to His Name; worship the Lord in Holy Array" (Ps. 29:1-2).

Solomon teaches that if we do, we need to take care with what we are going to do.

Read on.

Be Faithful to Your Vows, 5:4-7

"When you make a vow to God, do not be late in paying it; for He takes no delight in fools. Pay what you vow! It is better that you should not vow than that you should vow and not pay" (Eccl. 5:4-5). This is very similar to what Moses said in Deuteronomy 23:21-23: "Whatever your lips utter you must be sure to do, because you made your vow freely to the Lord your God with your own mouth" (*NIV*). Jesus made some strong statements about this in Matthew 5:33-37: "Again, you have heard that it was said to the people long ago, 'Do not break your oath, but keep the oaths you have made to the Lord.' But I tell you, Do not swear at all: either by heaven, for it is God's throne; or by the earth, for it is his footstool; or by Jerusalem, for it is the city of the Great King. And do not swear by your head, for you cannot make even one hair white or black. Simply let your 'Yes' be 'Yes,' and your 'No,' 'No'; anything beyond this comes from the evil one" (*NIV*).

Is Jesus saying that we should never make a vow to God nor promise Him anything? No, He's not saying that. The Apostle Paul made a vow and kept it (Acts 18:18). Jesus is talking to those who were swearing by everything and anything to give credibility to their integrity, i.e. their reputation was so ruined by their broken vows that they had to swear by something other than their own name. The Bible does not teach us to make vows to God but if we do, Solomon warns in Proverb 20:25: "It is a snare for a man to say rashly, 'It is holy!' and after the vows to make inquiry."

"Do not let your speech cause you to sin and do not say in the presence of the messenger of God that it was a mistake. Why should God be angry on account of your voice and destroy the work of your hands?" (Eccl. 5:6). While teaching that a tree is known by its fruit, Jesus says, "But I say that for every idle word men may speak, they will give account of it in the day of judgment. For by your words you will be justified and by your words you will be condemned" (Matt. 12: 36.37, *NKJV*). How can God be pouring His blessings upon you when He is struggling with your integrity? We talk about trusting God; the real question is can God trust you? Let me encourage you to take a moment and ask Jesus to forgive you for not following through on your past promises. Or maybe you need to ask His forgiveness for speaking idle words, lies, etc. Take a time for quiet confession right now.

"For in many dreams and in many words there is emptiness. Rather, fear God" (Eccl. 5:7). Rarely are our dreams useful, nor do most of them have anything to do with reality.[1] This is also the case with many words. Worship is not and should not be centered on us. Rather, the essence of true worship is to be "in Spirit and in Truth," dependant upon listening and responding to God. Fear God! Remember, when the terror is removed, reverence is left. It is in this state that we recognize His Lordship. "And Moses said to the people, 'Do not fear; for God has come to test you, and that His fear may be before you, so that you may not sin.' So the people stood afar off, but Moses drew near the thick darkness where God was" (Ex. 20:20-21, *NKJV*).

As we mentioned before, the New Testament concept of fearing God translates into faith. We worship in faith. We listen and pay attention to what He says and then, whatever we bring before Him is indeed worthy of His consideration.

The wisdom of worship is that when we make a vow telling Him we are going to do something, it is that vow that consumes us until we have completed our word.

In the 1990s, Matt Redman's song *"The Heart of Worship"* became somewhat of an anthem for many who sensed that worship in the Western church had become a bit too focused on performance. Redman says, "In some church services, it's obvious that the worship leader is consumed, above all else, with getting a response from the people. Not much is implied about the integrity and the heart of the offerings. Instead, comes a barrage of forceful encouragements to shout, clap, dance, or anything else you can think of."[2]

CHAPTER 11

The Illusions of Wealth
Ecclesiastes 5:8-17

—ᴟᴟ—

Economics can be bewildering. Like meteorologists, it seems that sometimes even the best of financial experts are not able to predict the ups and downs of the economy. The next natural disaster or terrorist attack could send the United Sates into a recession—some feel it's already here. Financially, things may get worse. Excluding the black horse of the Apocalypse, how tough is tough? (Rev. 6:5-6) When the next recession comes, what is it we have now that we won't have then? The answer? Money!

So much seems to wrap around the issue of money. We live in a world of "haves" and "have-nots." Most of us are a unique blend of both. But it looks like many of us could end up more on the "have-not" side. This, we determine, will be "tough times." I saw a cartoon that showed a man leaning up against his new sports car in front of a resort in his tennis attire with a supermodel hanging on his arm. The caption said, "I despise my life but I'm in love with my lifestyle." The truth is, money provides a lot of fun and experiences.

We are a culture of money thinking people. The 1980s introduced new terminologies for talking about ourselves. We called ourselves:

Yuppies:	Young urban professionals
Puppies:	Poor urban professionals
Buppies:	Black urban professionals
Grumpies:	Grown urban professionals
Dinks:	Double income, no kids
Silks:	Single income, lots of kids
Woofs:	Well-off older folks
Flyers:	Fun-loving youth en route to success

Does wealth really live up to its perceptions? Is it the key to warding off the tough times? Without it, will we be devoid of good times? In Ecclesiastes chapter 5, Kohelet reveals four illusions of wealth, if for no other reason than to spare you from the panic of not having it.

The "Have-Not's," 5:8-9

"If you see oppression of the poor and denial of justice and righteousness in the province, do not be shocked at the sight; for one official watches over another official, and there are higher officials over them" (Eccl. 5:8). If in this life, under this system, you're looking for justice and righteousness for all, don't hold your breath, you won't find it. Life isn't fair! Didn't your dad ever give you that speech? Injustice and unrighteousness are realities of this life "under the sun." Remember, they do not come from the Throne of God but from the thrones of men who rule this system. Because of this, there will always be the "have-nots." Solomon says there is another component that we should remember: there is one who is still sovereign over all of it. This phrase in the latter half of verse eight (8b) literally says, "A high one over a high one is watching and higher ones over them." We are

all accountable to other men, and these men are accountable to other men and… guess where it ultimately stops?

"After all, a king who cultivates the field is an advantage to the land" (Eccl. 5:9). The Message puts it this way, "But the good earth doesn't cheat anyone—even a bad king is honestly served by a field." With all the corruption and injustices of men, it is good to have someone, especially a leader, who is engaged in tilling the field, paying attention to what is happening and that "King" is best tied to verse 8—the King of kings, "Fear God!" Our culture believes that the only way to be delivered from tough times is to create good times. Is this accurate? There are four illusions of wealth and four things about money that are *not* true. By the way, the following insights are from the wealthiest man who ever lived.

The Illusions of the "Haves," 5:10-17

"He who loves money will not be satisfied with money, nor he who loves abundance with its income. This too is vanity" (Eccl. 5:10). "Call this toll-free number now and…you can be rich too!" Obviously, the cat is out of the bag with marketers that we want to be rich. There is an unending flow of infomercials telling us how to get rich by attending a seminar or workshop. It can happen for you! You can be rich!

First of all, what does it mean to be "satisfied?" The Hebrew word used here in verse 8 is *saba,* to have enough, to have one's fill. It is when you can say, "That's it, and I am content with my portion!"[1] We don't hear many people saying that do we?

It is a fact of life that we have some insatiable appetites (Eccl. 1:8). These appetites do not always make sense. Why are we like this? Why is simple contentment so elusive? We have an insatiable passion for money, another one of those great enigmas about us. And yet, notice the enigma is not the money itself or the abundance of it. Look at the verse closely, the "love" of it. *Aheb* is the same word used for the love of a friend; but what kind of a friend is money? John Rockefeller was asked once, "How much is enough?" To which he responded, "Just a little more." Why is that? It doesn't seem to make sense. That's why Solomon says, "This too is vanity," *hevel*, vaporous. The mystery of wealth is that, ultimately, it doesn't satisfy. If wealth is what you love, there will never be enough.

Does Wealth Provide Friends? "When good things increase, those who consume them increase. So what is the advantage to their owners except to look on?" (Eccl. 5:11). There's a principle of life in this verse and it goes like this: "The increase of goods means the increase of consumers." As is the case with lottery winners, the increase of wealth also produces an increase in claims upon that wealth. The more you have, the more you need to protect. Likewise, the more you have, the more you also have to distribute to those "friends" who are in need or have expectations.

Expectations can become your worst enemy. If you don't have anything, your friends know you can't do anything about their need. But what happens when they know you can do something about it and choose not to? If you don't do something to help, then your friends know that it's not because you couldn't, but it's only because you wouldn't. Will they trust that there's a good reason? Maybe. If you can and you don't, your friends want to know why you won't! Wealth doesn't add friends, it only adds consumers, those with the expectations and claims upon what you have.

Does Wealth Release Stress? "The sleep of the working man is pleasant, whether he eats little or much; but the full stomach of the rich man does not allow him to sleep" (Eccl. 5:12).

Stress is an interesting phenomenon. Stress effects sleep. We live in a society where 60 percent of the doctor visits in the United States are for signs of distress rather than a specific illness, where the top ten causes of death include only one infectious disease, and where the most highly prescribed drugs are tranquilizers. People need to be aware of stress and its effects.

Solomon contrasts the ease with which an exhausted worker falls asleep, even on a partially empty stomach, with the troubled thoughts of the wealthy. There's the man who works hard and can enjoy his rest. He puts in his eight hours, but then he leaves his work at work. He comes home and enjoys his family, his friends and an evening that includes some down time. The wealthy man's work tends to spill over into his personal life. When he gets home, he does a little more business related work, and later when his head hits the pillow he's thinking work-related thoughts: ("I wonder if the deal will go through?" "What if I don't get the position?" "What if they undercut my price and rip me off?" And/or, "How am I going to get out of this fix?"). Surprisingly, the accumulation of wealth actually *adds* stress to your life.

Does Wealth Give Security? "There is a grievous evil which I have seen under the sun: riches being hoarded by their owner to his hurt" (Eccl. 5:13). Solomon says there is a "grievous evil" which in the Hebrew is a "sickly evil." There is a "hurt" that can specifically affect the wealthy. Solomon provides us with the first of two evils that he has witnessed.

The first is the hoarding of wealth. Money is never utilized for pleasure, enjoyment, or even for charity.[2] Perhaps, the owner goes to extreme measures to protect it. I once heard a true story from a British pastor about a woman who lived on the streets as a homeless person. In fact, she would often beg just outside an Anglican church. She was killed in an altercation, and it was discovered shortly thereafter that she was the equivalent of a multi-millionaire. Those who knew her said that she was "saving up for a rainy day." The "rainy day" never came. She never enjoyed her wealth. Money can be a wicked mistress who takes from you more than she gives in return. The accumulation of wealth creates pain because the expectations of security from it are always disappointing.

"When those riches were lost through a bad investment and he had fathered a son, then there was nothing to support him. As he had come naked from his mother's womb, so will he return as he came. He will take nothing from the fruit of his labor that he can carry in his hand" (Eccl. 5:14-15). Wealth is sometimes transient, and it can be fickle. Solomon has revealed a "double-whammy" that is a part of wealth's DNA. The first nuisance is the acquiring of wealth and then there is the pain of losing it.

Let's take an interesting look back at the lives of nine the world's most successful financiers in the 1920's:[3]

- Howard Hopson—owner of AGECO, a conglomerate of electric and gas companies in New York, Ohio and Pennsylvania—*served a total of seven years in prison for mail fraud and tax evasion, lived out his life in obscurity and ill health.*
- Richard Whitney—Harvard-educated, president of the NYSE and a hero on "Black Thursday," the day of the stock market crash—*fell deep into debt from poor financial management and served three years in Sing Sing for grand larceny.*
- Arthur William Cutton—one of America's richest citizens and successful grain speculator—*suspected of being the ringleader of insider consortiums leading to the Great Crash of 1929; indicted for tax evasion.*
- Leon Fraser—a PhD grad from Columbia University; earned a Distinguished Service Cross in WW1; public servant; president of Bank for International Settlements; president of First National Bank of New York—*shot himself in the head because of depression.*
- Jesse Livermore—"Wall Street Wonder" and "Cotton King," multimillionaire and one of the most flam-

boyant and successful market speculators in the history of Wall Street—*committed suicide in 1940.*
- Albert Fall—New Mexico rancher; legislator; U.S. Senator; and Secretary of the Interior under President Warren G. Harding.—*implicated multiple times in government scandals and charges of conspiracy to defraud the government; convicted of bribery.*
- Ivar Kreuger—"Match King" and multibillionaire; ran a huge pyramid scheme, carefully avoiding financial audits—*financial crook of his era; investors lost millions in the largest bankruptcy of its time when his company went under. Kreuger shot himself or was murdered in 1932.*
- Samuel Insull—Assembled an empire of utility and transportation companies with holdings estimated around $3 billion—*lost his empire in the Great Depression; fled to Greece but was returned to stand trial for mail fraud, embezzlement and violation of bankruptcy acts; died at 78 in a Paris subway station with twenty cents in his pocket.*

Each of these men had learned and mastered the art of making a living, but not one of them had learned how to live! Solomon talks about a man who loses all he has and is robbed of a father's greatest joy: that of leaving something behind for his son. He came into this world with nothing, and leaves the same way. This is a very difficult concept for those of us who have spent most of our lives trying to accumulate something to hold in our hands. But there is nothing we can take with us in our hands. I have done a lot of funerals over the years, and I have never seen anything in a dead man's hand.

"This also is a grievous evil—exactly as a man is born, thus will he die? So what is the advantage to him who toils for the wind?" (Eccl. 5:16). Again he says, this is a "sickly evil"; literally it reads, "as he comes, he goes." We will all

suffer some sense of loss when we come to our deathbed. When we die, it will be the same as when we arrived, with nothing. So what's the use? Is all of it just "toil for the wind?" What's the "advantage" (*yitron*)? After you exceed your shelf life, what is left to enjoy? The sense of loss will have everything to do with the sense of gain you think you have now. You cannot take in your hand what is left over, but you *can* send it ahead. I'm talking about what Jesus said in Matthew 6:19-20, 24.

Years ago I saw a movie about the life of Jack Thum, a clown who lived in Chicago. The 1981 film was entitled *Leave 'em Laughing* with Mickey Rooney as Thum. As he lay in his hospital bed dying of lung cancer, he fought off depression, wondering if his life had meant anything. He loved people and had spent his life caring for homeless kids and making people laugh. It wasn't something he could take in his hand, but he had left a lot of other hands full. What about our hands, will they be empty? I often feel that our sense of time is distorted. We get confused about what time it is. We think time stands still for us, that there's never going to be a "then" because we have a "now." Delayed gratification isn't a popular concept. It doesn't fit well with our drive-thru mentality of instant gratification.

"Throughout his life he also eats in darkness with great vexation, sickness and anger" (Eccl. 5:17). Solomon reveals some ancient secrets by succinctly summarizing the four illusions of wealth.

1. Instead of satisfaction, it brings anxiety and vexation.
2. Instead of providing friends, it creates resentment because friends have become consumers.
3. Instead of relieving stress, there is sickness because of it.
4. Instead of giving security, there is darkness and fear.

The cost of wealth can be tragic. Now we can understand with more insight what Paul means in 1 Timothy 6:9: "But those who want to get rich fall into temptation and a snare and many foolish and harmful desires which plunge men into ruin and destruction."

CHAPTER 12

From the Hand of God
Ecclesiastes 5:18-20

—⁓—

There are a lot of things that come naturally to most of us. Why do you think that "gratefulness" happens *not* to be one of them? None of us would be comfortable being called an "ingrate," yet all the term means is not being grateful for the good in our lives. When it comes to gratefulness, we don't see much of it around, do we? There is a mindset that we should have the right to just about everything; its called "entitlement." From where did we get that thinking? At the core of it, you find a very simple, observable truth—if I have a need for something, I expect to have that need met. That is why we get angry or depressed when it isn't. We have many needs: physical, emotional, societal and professional. It is easy to become so preoccupied with ourselves and our needs while neglecting the needs and interests of others.

If we have convinced ourselves that we have the right to acquire anything we need, there isn't much room in our lives for gratefulness. Yet, did you know that in the Bible, "gratefulness" is actually commanded? Look at 1 Thessalonians 5:18. Why would God command us to give Him thanksgiving? The writer of Hebrews (13:15) says that "gratefulness" is the motivating force behind our worship. It isn't that God is insecure without it; it has something to do with us. Thanksgiving is God's will for our lives. *Ecclesiastes* provides us with a clue as to how we do it.

Remember what "joy" is? It's a sense of well-being because there's an absence of fear and a presence of hope. What causes "joy" to fade? Ready for this? The absence of "gratefulness!" Surprised? The key to "joy" is thanksgiving in *everything*. Only then are we reminded of His faithful care for us; thus, we need not fear the things around us. This is why it is "His will" that we give thanks lest any joy we would experience slip away.

I once heard the story about a man (we'll call him Joe) who was very disgruntled with his life. Primarily, he was unhappy with his wife and his job. Recent increases in property taxes had sent him into a tailspin of depression, so he made an appointment with his pastor. Prior to the meeting, his pastor had requested that Joe write down all of his disappointments. At the top of his list were: wife, job, and property taxes. As the meeting began, the pastor said to him, "I'm really sorry to hear about your wife passing away."

"What!?" Joe exclaimed! "What are you talking about? She just made me breakfast this morning"

"Oh, I see," said the pastor. "Well, I sure am sorry to hear that you got laid off."

"Laid off!" said Joe. "I didn't get laid off. I just received an increase in my salary at my last review, and the company I work for is doing well."

"Hmm. Well, Joe, I sure am sorry to hear that your house burned to the ground," said the pastor. At this point Joe figured out what was going on.

It's easy to forget God's blessings. For example, in Joe's case, there are many single men who would love to have a wife. No doubt at one time, I'm sure Joe was grateful that God had brought her into his life. Likewise, many people who are out of work would be very grateful to have Joe's job, his salary, and good marks on an annual performance review. Furthermore, many would love to live in the house and neighborhood with which he had been blessed.

A pursuit of life is not accumulation of wealth and possessions but rather the capacity to enjoy them no matter how great or how small. The key to enjoying them is "gratefulness."

Understanding the Wisdom of Grateful Living, 5:18

"Here is what I have seen to be good and fitting: to eat, to drink and enjoy oneself in all one's labor in which he toils under the sun during the few years of his life which God has given him; for this is his reward" (Eccl. 5:18). Do you remember the word "sage"? A prophet received the word of God and spoke it; a sage lived out his life, and God gave him insight into what living was all about. Knowledge came from the prophets, but wisdom from sages. What is "good and fitting"? The word "good" is *tov*, and it means "as it was designed to be enjoyed," sometimes translated "joyful." "Fitting" is that same word we saw in 3:11 — *Ya phah* — also translated "beautiful." This is the enjoyment of something without fear of anything being wrong with it (joyful and excellent).

Surprising as it may sound, God's desire is for us to joyfully enjoy what he has given us. This is not to be confused with the Greek Epicurean philosophy which Jesus credited the rich fool with saying in Luke 12:19, to "eat, drink and be merry for tomorrow we die." Enjoyment is not limited to merely eating and drinking but includes our work in producing, even our "toils under the sun," our hard work. You've probably thought about your blessings, but I'm guessing that hard work wasn't one of them. Can hard work be something enjoyable? When you know you are creating something good, you can feel as your Heavenly Father did when He created and then rested the seventh day. Failing to work hard is a cancer that brings misery to life. The biblical term is "sluggard." Solomon had a lot to say about the sluggard and the misery he brings upon himself. He is like a tragic comedy, and he is hinged to his bed (Prov. 26:14). His excuses are as ridiculous as "there is a lion outside" (Prov. 22:13).

A sluggard:
1. Will not begin things (Prov. 6:9-11).
2. Will not finish things (Prov. 19:24).
3. Is miserable (Prov. 13:4; 21:25-26).

God has designed us to work and to feel good about our work. The sluggard has failed to grasp that labor is a gift from the hand of God and that from this comes God's rewards and blessings in *this* life. He mentions the "few years God has given him." This is his reward and his share or portion. Most of us overlook this every time. The rewards are in the blessings of the labor and the fruit of our work. How do we ever learn to enjoy them?

But Grateful to Whom? 5:19
"Furthermore, as for every man to whom God has given riches and wealth, He has also empowered him to eat from them and to receive his reward and rejoice in his labor; this is the gift of God" (Eccl. 5:19). "God has given." We need to remember something here. It's the same thing Moses said in Deuteronomy 8:18: "But remember the Lord your God, for it is he who gives you the ability to produce wealth, and so confirms his covenant, which he swore to your forefathers, as it is today" (*NIV*). He has also "empowered" us to enjoy what He has given us. How? The Hebrew word *shalat* is a single word that means "to experience the enjoyment it was designed to give." We may not have as much as another, but we can learn to enjoy all of what we *do* have.

The point is that these are gifts from God. When we begin to see everything in terms of a gift from the hand of God, we will have acquired gratefulness. And where there is gratefulness, there will be joy. *"For he will not often consider the years of his life, because God keeps him occupied with the gladness of his heart" (Eccl. 5:20).*

People who have learned to enjoy life aren't focused on how much time they have left. A friend of mine shared with me how these verses had given her comfort during times of suffering with her serious liver disease. This is from a letter she wrote:

> *My frame of mind is described in verse 20 where it says. "For he will not often consider the years of his life, because God keeps him occupied with the gladness of his heart." This is precious, because it gives me permission not to feel guilty that I am not preoccupied and depressed by my situation. I also can say, yes, Lord, I see that it is you who occupies me with the gladness you have put in my heart, and it is ok!*

The wisdom of Solomon reveals that life is a joy and not a threat. God can make us sensitive to the goodness of life; and a proper understanding of Him and His plan for our lives can fill us with contentment. Have you asked God for this recently? By contrast, the fear of death inhibits those who have not learned to delight in the day. Have you ever been asked the question, "If you had only two weeks to live, what would you do?" Martin Luther was quoted as saying, "If I knew Jesus was to return tomorrow, I would still plant an apple tree today." God wants us to be about what he has given us to do. Listen carefully: When we acknowledge that what we have or do not have is from the hand of God, we are empowered to enjoy it's presence or absence.

Picture with me a conveyor belt with one apple passing by every twenty-four hours. Either we let it pass because we think there may be a better one coming, or we let it pass because we are distracted by previous ones we've enjoyed. Meanwhile, the one apple right in front of you passes untouched and "un-enjoyed." People are usually divided into three categories: Those who only know how to enjoy the past; those who only know how to anticipate the future; and those who have learned the wisdom of enjoying it all by living in the *moment!* The point is, life is enjoyed in the moment. The wisest thing you can do is to take the biggest bite of every apple that comes your way.

If you were going to teach someone to be grateful, what would you teach? Contrary to popular belief, the pursuit of life is *not* in accumulating wealth or possessions but learning how to enjoy what you have been given no matter how great or how small. The key is in seeing that what we already have are gifts from the hand of God. This leads to joy which in turn results in praise. This is when worship is genuine.

CHAPTER 13

Who Is Better Off? Part 1
Ecclesiastes 6:1-12

—ɯ—

Envy. We know what it feels like, and we know it's wrong, but do we know what it is? It's been defined as a feeling of discontent and ill will because of another's advantage. It's when we convince ourselves that those around us always have it better than we do. When the appearances are exposed, however, we are often surprised to learn that in actuality, we're not really missing out.

In Ecclesiastes 6, Solomon explains *why* there are apparent inequities. Does it seem at times that the other guy is always better off? God has a plan for our lives; but perhaps you are thinking, "I don't like my plan; can I trade it in for another?" It seems as if the other guy gets all the prosperity, and I get all the adversity. In Ecclesiastes 6 and 7, Solomon presents two important principles: First, prosperity is not always necessarily good; second, adversity is not always necessarily bad.

Those Outward Appearances, 6:1-2
"There is an evil which I have seen under the sun and it is prevalent among men" (Eccl. 6:1). I'm not a motivational

speaker, but I generally tend to be positive about life. In fact, I've even been told I can be obnoxiously cheerful. I have even had people in my life warn me about being *too* cheerful. I've been told, "Don't be too optimistic; the light at the end of the tunnel may well be another train!" I know this can be a frustrating and dangerous world, but some of us get stuck in our cynicism. Ralph Barton, the famous cartoonist, committed suicide and left this final commentary: "I have had few difficulties, many friends, great success; I have gone from wife to wife, and from house to house, visited great countries of the world, but I am fed up with inventing devices to fill up 24 hours of the day."

There is no question that we live in an unsafe world, but why do we allow it to rob us of the enjoyment of life? There will always be reasons to be cynical and bitter. The real world has some rotten stuff in it that brings pain and disappointment to all of us. The wisdom of Kohelet reveals that we need to interpret life in such a way that there can be joy and thanksgiving even in the midst of frustration and discouragement. It has everything to do with contentment (Phil. 4:11-12; 1 Tim. 6:6-8).

In Ecclesiastes 5:18, Solomon says it is "good and fitting" that we should enjoy all these good things God gives us with a "gladness of heart." Here he presents the flip side of what he has seen over the years as a sage: "an evil...prevalent among men," something that weighs heavily upon most. There is a reason he does not enjoy what he has been given, and Solomon is going to explain that the reason is failure to acknowledge that the gifts have come from the hand of God. *"A man to whom God has given riches and wealth and honor so that his soul lacks nothing of all that he desires; yet God has not empowered him to eat from them, for a foreigner enjoys them. This is vanity and a severe affliction"* *(Eccl. 6:2).* There are people who appear to have it all. They possess riches and wealth and all that money can buy. Our culture is obsessed with celebrities who seemingly have everything. In the same paper that carries information about critical national and world events, *USA Today* includes a "Life" section devoted to celebrity and entertainment news. Other publications such as *People* and *Us* provide a monthly update; and if that's not enough, we can get hourly coverage through the "Entertainment Channel." Why? Inquiring minds want to know because, for many Americans the "rich and famous" are the incarnation of their dreams. They seemingly have the life plan we want to live.

Solomon understood this. Solomon was able to accumulate for himself everything he wanted. No pleasure or possession was denied him. However, evidently God did not "empower" him to "eat from them" (5:19). Solomon had it made! But did he? Solomon says that "a foreigner enjoys [eats] them." So, you work for it, accumulate it, maintain it, insure it, and then someone else enjoys it. This is vaporous because when it passes on to the next generation, it doesn't always make sense; "it comes in futility and goes into obscurity." Having it can be a "severe affliction," but having it and not being able to enjoy it is worse than not having it at all. Why? Because he does not acknowledge that what he has was given to him from the hand of God (5:19, 20). This is the foolishness of the ungrateful.

Some Inward Realities, 6:3-6

"If a man fathers a hundred children and lives many years, however many they be, but his soul is not satisfied with good things and he does not even have a proper burial, then I say, 'Better the miscarriage than he'" (Eccl. 6:3). Because his soul is not satisfied with good things, even the blessings of more children or a longer life are unable to change anything. There is something inside that keeps him from being fulfilled. This is the curse of the "unsatisfied mind."

No matter how much wealth and honor you have acquired, if God has not empowered you to enjoy it, you will be empty.

As we learned earlier, if you do not acknowledge that these "good things" come from the hand of God, why would you expect God to give you the power to enjoy them? The outward appearance is that he "has it all"; but the inward reality is that he dies unfulfilled, unsatisfied, and unlamented. Solomon even goes so far as to compare the has-it-all man to a child's death at birth.

"For it comes in futility and goes into obscurity; and its name is covered in obscurity. It never sees the sun and it never knows anything; it is better off than he" (Eccl. 6:4-5). How can he say such a thing? Is this some horrible cynical remark?

This is the stillborn child; he comes in futility (*hevel*) like a vapor that passes away quickly and, thus, into obscurity. The child's identity and personality and all it would have been is covered, and no one will ever know him. Then Solomon uses the metaphor of never seeing the sun. The child will never experience all the things life has to offer. Yet, Solomon says that the stillborn is better off[1] than the man who has it all and is unable to enjoy it. Is this simply the use of hyperbole? What does he mean by this? Although the stillborn child missed all the pleasures of life, the child also missed all the suffering and disappointments of life as well.

"Even if the other man lives a thousand years twice and does not enjoy good things—do not all go to one place?" (Eccl. 6:6). A long life is a joy only to those who have learned to enjoy it. A longer life, in and of itself, is not a blessing. As one medical physician put it, "Medical science is giving us longer life but no reason to live." The unsatisfied mind is unable to find enjoyment or to see the good things. Ironically, the one who has it all may not be able to see them as the "good things" of his life. It is as if his eyes pass right over them to something else that doesn't exist in his life; so

both he and the stillborn child die. Who is better off? The man who went to the grave with the pain of knowing he missed the whole point of living or the child who missed only the suffering of that living?

So, do we still want to argue with God about the plan? The more we study life, the more our mumblings become awkward and even embarrassing to us.

Some Awkward Arguments, 6:7-12

"All a man's labor is for his mouth and yet the appetite is not satisfied" (Eccl. 6:7). What if we work harder? Maybe that would change the plan and make it more the way we want it to be. The Hebrew word for "appetite" is *nephesh,* the same word used in Genesis 2:7, "a living being." The "being" or "soul" of a man is not satisfied with more and, therefore, exerting more work to provide for it is foolish.

"For what advantage does the wise man have over the fool?" (Eccl. 6:8a). "Maybe I should become smarter and more educated. Perhaps degrees would provide me with the things that would satisfy." Ultimately, more intelligence or education still isn't going to help. In some cases it may even make you more cynical; thus, more miserable (Ecclesiastes 1:18). By the way, if you would like to know what it's like to be more educated than everyone, simply spend an entire day with some preschoolers. You'll get a pretty good idea of how much fun it is to be the brightest.

"What advantage does the poor man have, knowing how to walk before the living?" (Eccl. 6:8b). Does this mean that we should quit work and take a vow of poverty? Nothing is wrong with simplifying your life; but Solomon is saying that if you have an "unsatisfied mind," what makes you think you will enjoy the little when you could not enjoy the much?

"What the eyes see is better than what the soul desires. This too is futility and a striving after wind" (Eccl. 6:9). Commenting on this verse, Chuck Swindoll chides, "Don't

hitch your wagon to the stars of your imagination!" Come to terms with reality. What you are able to see is better than all of the dreams you hope for and believe are out there just waiting for you. People die in their fantasies, missing out on enjoying the life that God has given them. They are unable to see the blessings of life right under their noses.

"Whatever exists has already been named, and it is known what man is; for he cannot dispute with him who is stronger than he is" (Eccl. 6:10). All things are "named and known." The plan is the plan. At the heart of our struggle over the equity of plans is a theological issue: Do we really believe that God has our best interests at heart? Trusting that God knows us and what's best for us is a key component in being able to not only seize the day, but to seize the life! If we don't like the plan, or can't change the plan, then some of us attempt to change God.

We should not try to change who God is simply because we do not understand the plan. God is sovereign and we are not. Quarreling with Him is a waste of time. Remember, we have finite minds trying to fully understand the infinite. We have asked the question before—isn't it logical that squeezing infinite thinking into finite creates some spillage and that this spillage can be called reasonable mystery?

As long as we fight the hand of God, we fail to apprehend Him, and life will not be smooth. As the late Corrie Ten Boom described it, the tapestry from underneath is full of knots and twisted threads and frayed ends that lack meaning and beauty.

Not till the loom is silent and the shuttles cease to fly
Will God unroll his canvas and explain the reason why.
The dark threads are as needful in the weaver's
skillful hands
As the threads of gold and scarlet in the pattern
he has planned.

Perhaps you are wondering, "Is this defeatism, fatalism, or is it realism?" However, the real question should be: Who is sovereign, God or me? We need to determine at the very core of our being what we believe about this.

"For there are many words which increase futility. What then is the advantage to a man?" (Eccl. 6:11). The point is, when are you going to stop arguing with God over the plan for your life? Sure we can (and should) express our requests and our desires (Phil. 4:6), but we are not to mock His wisdom by mocking His plan. This returns us to what Solomon said at the beginning of the book. *"Vanity of vanities,"* says Kohelet. Life is vaporous; it passes quickly and doesn't always make sense to us. It's like taking a novel and opening to a random page, reading it, and trying to make sense out of the entire story. We simply do not have the proper understanding of God. God is able to speak galaxies into existence. He is able to say "Let there be light" and there is light! We have finite minds. He has infinite wisdom. He is omniscient; we have a three-pound brain. Simply put, there are some things in life that we simply cannot understand. There is no debate in my head about this yet, at times, there is a real struggle in my heart. It is at these times that I take comfort in the fact that God is good (Ps. 103).

"For who knows what is good for a man during his lifetime, during the few years of his futile life? He will spend them like a shadow. For who can tell a man what will be after him under the sun?" (Eccl. 6:12). Because life passes quickly, it can be spent on shadows, pursuing things that are not real. How often have you said, "If only I could have... then I would be happy"? How often have you received it only to discover that it didn't make you happy.

Who is better off? Who ended up with the best plan? The "unsatisfied mind" will rob you of all the good things that come with God's plan for you and your life. If you pursue the plans of others, you will come up empty because God's plan for someone else is only an illusion for you (Eccl. 6:9). What is real for you? It's right in front of you! The question is, how do you live it out?

CHAPTER 14

Who Is Better Off? Part 2
Ecclesiastes 7:1-8

—ᴍᴜ—

B eginning with chapter 7, Solomon explains the apparent inequities we see in the different plans God has for different people. As we have already learned, life is a gift from the hand of God; and there is a plan for each one of us. But life doesn't always seem like a gift for some. In fact, maybe you feel that if your current plan is a gift from God then, please—no more gifts! How can I get excited about God's plan for my life when it appears as if everyone else's plan is better than mine? At some point, most of us wish we could trade in our plan for another.

In the previous section, we discussed our "nose problems." We stick our noses into the gift bags of others and compare them unfavorably to our own. The reason we tend to believe that others are better off is because of the adversities our bags contain. "Why does he get all the good and I get all the bad?" Yet, the one with the adversity just may have the greater good because of the bad—what are we getting at here? The point of this passage is that adversity can have the greater beneficial effect on us, even more so than prosperity. If we are ever going to reconcile the ways of God with our disappointments, it needs to happen with *this* issue: How do I view hardship?

In the first eight verses of chapter 7, Solomon gives us seven "better thans…" These are what we call proverbs, short pointed statements of raw truth; no arguments, no explanations, no justification, just simply raw truth!

1. "But" — Sometimes they come in the form of *contrastive statements.* They contrast two things: "A wise son heeds his father's instruction, *but* a mocker does not listen to rebuke" (Prov. 13:1).
2. "And" — Sometimes they take the form of *completive statements* like Proverbs 1:8, "Listen, my son, to your father's instruction *and* do not forsake your mother's teaching."
3. "Better than" — Other times they come as *comparative statements:* A is better than B. There are seven of these comparative statements within these eight verses. He begins with…

A Good Name Is Better Than…, 7:1a

"A good name is better than a good ointment" (Eccl. *7:1a).* The Hebrew has a play on words here (*tov shem mishemen tov*). The Hebrew word for "name" is *shem* and *shemen* is the word for "perfume." Solomon is saying a good *shem* is better than a good *shemen.* Perfume attracts and it catches attention. If we believe the advertisements, it is amazing what a little aroma can do; women lose control and men become sensitive and romantic. Solomon is saying if you want to be attractive, there is something better than perfume: it is a "good name." In Proverbs, Solomon says: "A good name is more desirable than great riches; to be esteemed is better than silver or gold" (Prov. 22:1). Your name is how you are known—what kind of person you are. You may say, "I don't care what people think of me." Maybe you don't,

but as a child of God, you should care because God does. God is concerned about your name because it reflects on His own (Ezek. 36:22-23). It is a good name that attracts others and gives the credibility to what we say.

What does this have to do with adversity? A good name hinges on how we handle adversity. Hardship has a way of revealing who we really are. I've always said that if you want to know what someone is like, bump them and see what spills out. True character is revealed through adversity. If you want to know what people are really like, watch them when times are tough. The strength of the fiber is seen only when that fiber is stretched.

When Death Can Be Better Than Birth, 7:1b

"And the day of one's death is better than the day of one's birth" (Eccl. 7:1b). Initially, this appears to be a little existentialist doesn't it? I mean, we celebrate birthdays but mourn when someone dies, so what is Solomon saying? A secret of Kohelet is that the question of who we really are is not settled until we die. The book is finished only when the last chapter has been written. The character of a person is seen in the context of his *entire* life. Maybe you were a wonderful child, a delightful young man, an admirable middle-aged woman, but how did you finish your life? Your greatest influence will probably be after the whole story is written and the book is finally published for all to read.

Another reason death is better than birth is because you can leave the labor of life behind. The fears and uncertainties and storms are successfully battled and have been won. When Pastor Les Hughey lost a friend named Larry, he was asked to sing at the memorial service. He sat down and wrote this song:

It's taken a long time for me to see
That death is not bad like I thought it would be.

127

It's the best part of God's plan;
He takes us to his land.
It is a blessing to be in the presence of God eternally!
To live is Christ, but to die is gain.
We shall not fear, we are not slain.
It's what we've waited for;
We walk right through the door.
Don't you wish that you could be
In the presence of God eternally?
Don't you wish that you were happy like Larry?

When Mourning Is Better Than Feasting, 7:2

"It is better to go to a house of mourning, than to go to a house of feasting, because that is the end of every man, and the living takes it to heart" (Eccl. 7:2). When we are confronted with death, there is a focus that automatically filters out meaningless distractions. Death has an uncanny way of making us look at life. Though it brings sorrow, grief, and mourning, you set aside the shallow aspects of life and deal with the facts of reality. There is a need for "sobriety" in our lives. Do you know what "sobriety" is? It's not the opposite of being "wasted." Sobriety speaks of the seriousness that surrounds us. Like Peter Pan, sometimes we don't want to deal with the consequences of growing up. There is a time for feasting but if that is all there is, we will be as shallow as a thimble. Because of our values, facing our mortality will change who we are. There is a sense of passage into maturity. Let me ask you a couple of questions: When you realize that death is around the corner what will become important to you? Why are those things not important now?

When Sorrow Is Better Than Laughter, 7:3-4

"Sorrow is better than laughter, for when a face is sad a heart may be happy. The mind of the wise is in the house of mourning, while the mind of fools is in the house of pleasure"

(Eccl. 7:3-4). You can't be serious! You really expect me to believe that sorrow produces more gladness than laughter? How can that be? Perhaps Solomon has slipped a synapse![1]

I know what you're thinking. First, Solomon has us considering that the lifestyle of the rich and famous isn't all it's made out to be and that death is better than birth; but now it appears he's gone too far.

What exactly does he mean by "sorrow"? A *thoughtful* sadness is a reflection over those things that have caused the pain. This has a way of purifying the heart and making it glad. First, it creates sensitivity to others who are hurting. Second, it is the wise mind that understands what evil is and the pain it creates. The fool, however, only desires to escape and run from his pain (or drown it in pleasure). Because the fool fails to learn from his sorrows, he will continue to bring that same pain upon himself and others again and again, over and over. Solomon puts it less delicately in his proverb, "As a dog returns to his vomit so does a fool to his folly" (Prov. 26:11). Sorrow is sacred. Sorrow beautifies the soul. Sorrow makes wise.

When Rebuke Is Better Than Songs, 7:5-7

"It is better to listen to the rebuke of a wise man than for one to listen to the song of fools" (Eccl. 7:5). Who will tell you the truth, even when it wounds deeply? (see Prov. 27:5-6; 28:23). It is always painful to be corrected. It's a shot to the ego and is quite frankly humiliating.

What is rebuke? Is there any difference between rebuke and criticism? Rebuke is grave admonishment which heals and strengthens while it wounds. Proverbs 17:10 says, "A rebuke impresses a man of discernment more than a hundred lashes to a fool." Rebuke wounds and heals, but criticism just wounds! Obviously, I would rather have nice people sing songs about me and pretend that everything wrong with me will just go away; just laugh it off. But remember, we are looking at comparative statements. Simple facts. And the fact is that receiving a rebuke from the wise is the better of the two options.

"For as the crackling of thorn bushes under a pot, so is the laughter of the fool; and this too is futility" (Eccl. 7:6). In the Hebrew, there is another play on words here. It might be translated, "as the crackling of nettles under kettles." Songs and laughter quickly kindle and blaze up for a time with a lot of noise and heat; but they soon die away. So it is with all the strokes we beg for when it is rebuke we actually need.

"For oppression makes a wise man mad, and a bribe corrupts the heart" (Eccl. 7:7). This "oppression" is not our suffering but rather the oppression we give out. This is a warning that all of us need rebuke, especially those in positions of authority and power who can oppress others. A man without accountability will go mad without rebuke. He will no longer know how to wield his authority with reason and sensitivity. A bribe or gift corrupts the heart. We can be swayed with gifts and our authority can be perverted. No man or woman is above rebuke and a "good name" will be destroyed without it.

When the Ending Is Better Than the Beginning, 7:8a

"The end of a matter is better than its beginning" (Eccl. 7:8a). The beginning of things can be frightening especially when the ending is uncertain. Many times painful beginnings only make sense after the whole picture has been painted. You have heard it said that "hindsight is 20/20," so wise foresight would begin with asking questions of those with the hindsight.

When Patience Is Better Than Haughtiness, 7:8b

"Patience of spirit is better than haughtiness of spirit" (Eccl. 7:8b). What is patience? In this case, it literally means "long of spirit" contrasted with "short in spirit" used

in Proverbs 14:29. How long does it take for you to get angry? "Haughtiness" is an inflated ego compounded with pride. It results in thinking that everything must be arranged according to my control or manipulation, and ignores God's providence. Why do we want to control? Typically we want control because we want circumstances to our own liking and preferences within our own domain. Yet, it's really not our domain. It is God's domain! The Bible says, "The earth is the Lord's and all it contains, the world and all who dwell in it" (Ps. 24:1).

Adversity just may be the best thing you ever found in your bag!

CHAPTER 15

Wisdom to the Wise
Ecclesiastes 7:9-14

—∿—

To some, education is the most important commitment of their energy while others rarely give it much thought. If you ask people about their education, they will quickly give you their academic pedigree. We want to be educated because we all want to be smart, but when does our education stop? What grade are you in these days? The accumulation of wisdom is just the continuation of your post-graduate work of life. But some are failing the "School of Real World" too quickly. Wisdom is only to the wise. In other words, unless we become wise in a few things, we'll never become wise unto wisdom. We need to wise up (pun intended) to the reason some of us aren't growing in wisdom. It has to do with not wising up to the very things that block growth in wisdom. Here are some roadblocks that can stunt our growth in wisdom.

Wisdom's Great Hurdle Is Anger, 7:9

"Do not be eager in your heart to be angry, for anger resides in the bosom of fools" (Eccl. 7:9). Solomon says don't be hasty to get angry. We talked briefly about this in

chapter 7:8. To be "short in spirit" is to be "short in sense." Don't be in a hurry to get mad at the way things are when they aren't the way you want them to be.

God has given us emotions for a good reason. He created us in His image and as He has emotions, so do we. Our English word "emotion" is from a Latin word that is linked to "movement." The word "emotion" means to move out. The purpose of our emotion is to generate energy within us to do something. If we were without emotions, we would be lifeless, having no desires or motivation. Picture yourself as a blob with nothing but a few reflexes to identify you as being alive.

Anger is an interesting emotion. Are there ever occasions when it's right to get angry? Ephesians 4:26-27 says, "Be angry, and yet do not sin; do not let the sun go down on your anger, and do not give the devil an opportunity." In verse 31, Paul goes on to say "Get rid of all bitterness, rage and anger, brawling and slander, along with every form of malice" (*NIV*). In Proverbs 25:28, Solomon says, "Like a city whose walls are broken down is a man who lacks self-control" (*NIV*).

Emotions generate energy. For example:

1. The emotion of fear generates the energy to protect.
2. The emotion of affection generates the energy to serve.
3. The emotion of sorrow initiates reflection and contemplation.
4. The emotion of anger generates the energy to correct things that are wrong.

Within the context of Ephesians 4 and 5, we are instructed to correct evil when we see it (Ephesians 5:11), and we are to correct it quickly (not letting the sun go down, 4:26).

A life incapable of anger is a life destitute of the needful energy to correct what is wrong in this world. The Holy Spirit makes us capable of healthy heat, and He inspires the fire within.

But when is anger destructive? Ephesians 4:31 tells us that anger is destructive when it is a result of bitterness which is another word for resentment.

I remember hearing James Dobson discuss the topics of stress and burnout. According to his studies, anger due to bitterness was the number one cause for burnout. When my expectations are not met, when my world is not the way I want it, I resent it; and if this is from where my anger is coming, then it will block wisdom from coming into my life. Solomon says, "Anger resides in the bosom of fools" (Eccl. 7:9).

Wisdom's Other Great Hurdle Is Discontentment, 7:10

"Do not say, 'Why is it that the former days were better than these? For it is not from wisdom that you ask about this" (Eccl. 7:10). What does this have to do with discontentment? We forget to remember the pain of the past. We either repress it or just choose to pretend there were no adversities in our life. Once the past is purged of the hard times, we even romanticize it and refer to "the good old days." The result is discontentment with the present. We are left believing there was a time of no disappointments and that life now is worse than it ever was before. In reality the good old days are the "here and now." Psalm 118:24 says, "This is the day the Lord has made; let us rejoice and be glad in it" (*NIV*). (See also Phil. 4:10-13.) Discontentment is not a byproduct of wisdom, for it is an escape from being wise about the present. That is why it blocks what you could be learning from the present. Stay with the plan and the plan is now.

What Is the Great Worth of Wisdom? 7:11-14

It begins with protection... "Wisdom along with an inheritance is good and an advantage to those who see the sun" (Eccl. 7:11). "Along with" is actually just one word in the Hebrew and may also be translated into the English word "as" meaning that wisdom is as good "as" an inheritance. It is something that is passed on from generation to generation, and it gives an advantage to those "who see the sun," those who live out their lives. What advantage?

"For wisdom is protection just as money is protection, but the advantage of knowledge is that wisdom preserves the lives of its possessors" (Eccl. 7:12). Literally, the sentence reads: "in the shade is wisdom, in the shade is money." In other words, with wisdom and money you've got it made in the shade. "Shade" to the oriental mind meant protection; protection from what? Protection from destroying yourself. The clue is that wisdom, like money, provides a particular kind of refuge. This is similar to Proverbs 13:8, "A man's riches may ransom his life, but a poor man hears no threat." In ancient times, as well as today, money can get you out of trouble. Likewise, wisdom can protect you from serious harm. Fools destroy themselves. Not only do fools destroy themselves but those who associate with them. Proverbs 13:20 says, "He who walks with the wise grows wise, but a companion of fools suffers harm" (*NIV*).

What is the difference between knowledge and wisdom? Some feel there is no difference in these terms but that they are varied only for the sake of poetic expression. I believe there is a distinction. *Da at* (knowledge) speaks of understanding what is good and what is evil. *Hokmah* (wisdom) speaks of skill; a kind of intelligence that can range from artistic to relational. *Da at* and *hokmah* are two sides of the same thing. You begin with knowledge and end with wisdom (Col. 1:9-10). Knowledge is the revelation of what is true.

Wisdom, however, is the *skill to apply it*. One is about knowing, the other is about living it out.

...*and ends with perspective*. *"Consider the work of God, for who is able to straighten what He has bent?" (Eccl. 7:13)*. Instead of getting angry and discontent over your situation, consider something. You take the good things from the hand of God without argument, then why not the bad things? For who is able to straighten what God has bent? The presence of afflictions and adversities in life are also part of His plan for you. You may not always understand or like what you find in your bag, but it's been placed there for a reason. In the New Testament, we are instructed by James to "count it all joy, my brothers, when you meet trials of various kinds, for you know that the testing of your faith produces steadfastness" (Jas. 1:2-3 *ESV*). Like clay in the hand of the potter, we can take solace in the fact that when God is doing the twisting and the shaping, it is for our own good (Rom. 8:28). Therefore, we can trust the Potter.

"In the day of prosperity be happy, but in the day of adversity consider—God has made the one as well as the other so that man will not discover anything that will be after him" (Eccl. 7:14). There will be those times of no adversity; I call those times "breathing points." When they come along, don't feel guilty about them. The rendering here of the text is "in the day of good be in good." When things go well with you, rejoice and celebrate. Do you know how to celebrate good times? You're not saying everything is perfect, but you are saying I am grateful things are good right now. What Solomon is telling us to consider is this: "God has made the one as well as the other so that man may not discover anything that will be after him." They both come from God, the good times and the bad times!

Remember Job? Everything that happened to him (the good and the bad) first passed through God's throne room (Job 2:9-10). As Oswald Chambers said, "A saint's life is in the hands of God like a bow and arrow in the hands of an archer. God is aiming at something the saint cannot see, but our Lord continues to stretch and strain, and every once in awhile the saint says, 'I can't take any more.' Yet God pays no attention; He goes on stretching until His purpose is in sight, and then He lets the arrow fly."[1]

The issue of wisdom is: do we believe God has any of it? God mingles the good with the bad in our lives according to a wisdom we cannot attain to in this life. We are not to forecast our future through horoscopes or psychics. Rather, our dependence is in God.

We need to look with wonder and admire silently as we wait for the result of God's work. The disparity in life is allowed by God so that we might ultimately develop a simple trust and dependence on Him. Prosperity and the good come from God's hand; be thankful. But in adversity and the crookedness of life, reflect on the goodness of God and the comprehensiveness of his plan for men.

How will you ever begin to understand how adversity can work for your good if you are always getting mad or trying to escape from it? Is it possible to ever understand it? James says God is willing to give you some wisdom in understanding if you are asking with a heart that is honest and not a raised fist. In his book, *Holy Sweat*, Tim Hansel tells the story of a man walking across the desert stumbling, almost dying of thirst, when he sees a well. As he approaches the well, he finds a note in a can close by. The note reads: "Dear Friend, there is enough water in this well, enough for all, but sometimes the leather washer gets dried up and you have to prime the pump. Now if you look underneath the rock just west of the well, you will find a bottle full of water, corked. Please don't drink the water. What you've got to do is take the bottle of water and pour the first half very slowly over the washer to loosen the leather. Then pour the rest in very fast and pump like crazy! You will get water. The well has never run dry. Have faith, and when you're done, don't forget to put the note back, fill up the bottle and put it back under the rock. Good Luck and have a fun trip, sincerely your friend, Desert Pete."[2] Would you "have faith"? There is a point where you have to start trusting someone!

Wisdom is to the wise. Anger and discontentment will alienate you from it. Without wisdom you'll never learn your spiritual A-B-Cs. Knowledge knows right from wrong while wisdom understands why. Wisdom is that art of knowing how to live out life as God designed it to be enjoyed. Do you desire to be wise? What's preventing you—what's your hurdle?

CHAPTER 16

Too Righteous for Your Own Good

Ecclesiastes 7:15-18

—ᴡᴡ—

We abstain from certain endeavors—like drunkenness, stealing, and infidelity—because we are Christians; *or* are we Christians because we abstain from those things? How much of what we do or not do as believers has to do with the Spirit of God within us? And how much of what we do or not do has to do with what others think of us? Do we want to be righteous? Some of us desire so strongly to be righteous that we even begin to hurt ourselves with a "strained righteousness." Others don't try at all because they've convinced themselves that good has no enjoyment to it. Where does honest godliness come in?

There Is a Strained Righteousness, 7:15-16

"I have seen everything during my lifetime of futility; there is a righteous man who perishes in his righteousness and there is a wicked man who prolongs his life in his wickedness. Do not be excessively righteous and do not be overly wise. Why should you ruin yourself?" (Eccl. 7:15-16). Solomon is writing this toward the end of his life and

reflecting on what he has seen as he has observed people in his lifetime. He refers to his life as "a lifetime of futility." Again, the word is *hevel* (vaporous and, thus, puzzling). At times *hevel* moments appear senseless and may disturb our sense of what is right and fair, even to the point of questioning God's sense of justice and righteousness.

Several years ago I read *The 12th of August*, which was based on the life of Buford Puzzer, better known from the film adaptation, *Walking Tall*. For those of you unfamiliar with the plot, it is based on the true story of sheriff Puzzer's futile attempt to single-handedly battle corruption in a small town. Solomon also sees something disturbing: "...a righteous man who perishes in his righteousness." Good people sometimes suffer and sometimes die. It doesn't seem right! The context of verses 13 and 14 has already made the observation that God works in a manner that doesn't always make sense to us.

If that is not enough frustration, there is also the wicked who seem to be blessed with a long and prosperous life. Like the psalmist, I hate it when the bad guys win (Ps. 73:11-17).

As reflected in comic books and movies, most of us were raised with the expectation that the good guys win in the end. Eventually, however, from *Walking Tall*, we see that reality doesn't always reflect this. This is why some of us get a little confused. If that is real life, why be good if good guys don't always win? Why bother if there are no guarantees?

"Do not be excessively righteous and do not be overly wise. Why should you ruin yourself?" That is a raw proverb! What in the world is he talking about, "Do not be excessively righteous or overly wise?" He is talking about the fact that people are creatures of extremes. We either go one way or the other. If I am going to be good then I am going to be good at being good. We fall into the trap so easily. This is what Jesus was talking about in Luke 5:32 when he said, "I have not come to call righteous men but sinners to repentance." The Scribes and the Pharisees had convinced themselves they were as good as good could be (Matt. 5:20).

A "strained righteousness" produces an arrogance and conceit to the point that one begins to question God's righteousness when it doesn't match up with their own. This self-effort righteousness is nothing more than self-righteousness. This leads to being "overly wise," matching your wisdom with His and believing you are the brighter of the two. (See Mal. 2:17; 3:13-15.)

Kohelet says, "Why ruin yourself?" Why get a spiritual hernia? Your pursuit of righteousness may destroy the very character of true righteousness. Be careful that you do not become merely religious. So, how are we to pursue righteousness in a healthy manner? What's your purpose in it? This is where the Pharisees got into trouble. They focused so hard on the externals that they missed the personal God. Their religion surpassed the presence of God. But then there's the other extreme that is also dangerous.

And There Is a Relaxed Wickedness, 7:17

"Do not be excessively wicked and do not be a fool. Why should you die before your time?" (Eccl. 7:17). Excessively wicked? Is it okay to be just a *little* wicked? Or maybe sin is okay as long as it's in moderation? This would obviously be inconsistent with the admonitions seen in Leviticus 19:2, "Be holy, for I the Lord your God am holy," and quoted by Peter in 1 Peter 1:16. Solomon, however, is using a grammatical structure to provide contrast between the two extremes; thus, he is teaching that not only should we avoid excessive righteousness, but we should also avoid excessive wickedness. Both of these extremes are trademarks of a "fool," but *excessive* wickedness can result in a premature destruction of life and bring about your own demise. Be wise in your choices!

"When I pondered to understand this [the prosperity of the wicked], it was troublesome in my sight until I came into the sanctuary of God; then I perceived their end (Ps. 73:16-17).

CHAPTER 17

What's Wrong with Me?
Ecclesiastes 7:19-29

—⁓—

Have you ever noticed that we don't always do things right? A little insensitivity here, a little offense there, a little indifference here, a little anger there; even when we try to do it right, it doesn't always come together. We get frustrated, and we don't understand. Why don't they understand what I'm trying to do? Why don't they understand me? The answer isn't really very difficult. Why do we expect people to understand us when, in truth, we don't really understand ourselves?

Many Americans spend a lot of time and money on self-analysis. This can be helpful for discovering the catalyst for some of our problems. Personally, from my experience in pastoral counseling, I have noticed that many of these cases involved people who were simply unhappy. Self-hate has never been a means to physical or spiritual health. In those quiet moments of solitude, and after you have blamed everyone else for your problems, have you ever asked yourself, "What's wrong with me?"

The elementary problem is that we don't like the idea that we have a problem. We have mastered self-justification to the point that we never ask ourselves the question. But if we never ask it of ourselves, then we will continue the rest of our lives with an unsolvable problem.

We've Got a Problem! 7:19-22

"Wisdom strengthens a wise man more than ten rulers who are in a city" (Eccl. 7:19). We learned from the previous chapter that wisdom is the skill of living a life of reverence for God (v.18). Reverence is the result of being in awe of God. This produces a desire to please Him. It is this deep desire to please God that keeps us on the right path between moral legalism and moral indifference (i.e., strained righteousness and relaxed wickedness).

Can you imagine how insightful it would be to access an executive think tank? Solomon teaches that wisdom actually strengthens a wise man more effectively than any advisory board. You can get all the advice you desire from the brightest of counselors; yet this particular problem has to do with something in you they will never understand, and only the wisdom of God will make any sense out of it for you.

"Indeed, there is not a righteous man on earth who continually does good and who never sins" (Eccl. 7:20). When we try to put handles on the problem, the first thing we must acknowledge is that we are sinners. There are great people and humanitarians who have devoted most of their lives to just and noble causes and yet, they are sinners. This verse is similar to what Paul said to the church in Rome, "There is none righteous, no not one" (Rom. 3:10). An excess of good deeds doesn't cancel out sins. Can I murder someone and then do community service for their family?

The Bible records this about our problem:

- "Who can say, 'I have kept my heart pure; I am clean and without sin?'" Proverbs 20:9.

- "All of us have become like one who is unclean, and all our righteous acts are like filthy rags; we all shrivel up like a leaf, and like the wind our sins sweep us away," Isaiah 64:6.
- "For all have sinned and fall short of the glory of God," Romans 3:23.

Do you know what sin is? First John 3:4 tells us that everyone breaks the law of God. That is sin.

Have you ever told a lie?
You've broken the Law: "Thou shall not lie" (Exod. 20:16).
Have you ever stolen something?
You've broken the Law: "Thou shall not steal" (Exod. 20:15).

Shall I continue? Sin separates us from God. This separation and indifference is our problem. God created life, and indifference to His plan for our lives is logically absurd. That is why we see such absurdity around us

"Also, do not take seriously all words which are spoken, so that you will not hear your servant cursing you" (Eccl. 7:21). Our mouths are often "exhibit A" of our problem (Jas. 3:2). For example, when people slander one another, it serves as evidence for the existence of sin. Solomon's counsel is to choose to see it for what it really is: a demonstration of the problem of sin. Some of us always want to know, "What are people saying about me?" This is not a healthy practice. First, because it establishes a false standard that will choke you to death. Second, it will control you like a puppet on strings. David had some good advice on this as well: "I am like a deaf man, who cannot hear, like a mute, who cannot open his mouth" (Ps. 38:13).

"For you also have realized that you likewise have many times cursed others" (Eccl. 7:22). Occasionally, I have found myself sucked into conversations that are unwholesome and demeaning of others. There is no excuse for this because much of what you hear isn't complete truth and is misspoken in foolishness.

Don't be surprised and don't overreact when it happens, because you are as guilty as anyone else. We prove the point: we all have the same problem. We get mad and speak pejoratively of others, even when we like them. The problem of sin is within us, not outside of us. Let's just admit it to each other. Our nature is to be indifferent to God and indifferent to His wisdom and purpose for our lives. When we slander or are slandered, it reminds us of the spiritual virus of sin.

The Problem Is With Us! 7:23-28

"I tested all this with wisdom, and I said, 'I will be wise,' but it was far from me. What has been is remote and exceedingly mysterious who can discover it?" (Eccl. 7:23-24). We can discover many things about our world, but there is still the mystery of it all that confounds the wisest. This is one facet I actually like about the postmodern era: mystery. It is okay that we cannot figure everything out. "I don't know" is an acceptable and authentic response these days. In some ways, Solomon was ahead of his time. Solomon said, "I wanted to be wise," to figure out everything in life; but the greatest enigma I found was me.

"I directed my mind to know, to investigate and to seek wisdom and an explanation, and to know the evil of folly and the foolishness of madness" (Eccl. 7:25). Why do we do it? What is it in the character of a man that keeps us from seeing the "evil," the "folly" and the "foolishness" in the "madness"? Technically, "folly" means to be "plump in the head." I was taught not to use the word "stupid," but "stupid" is the correct translation of this Hebrew word. It means to

live in a state of being in a stupor: dazed, dulled, and without understanding. "Madness" means unable to use your mind because your emotions have hijacked your reasoning. We are blind to the consequences of this madness because we live more in the natural rather than the supernatural realm. Rarely do we break through to wisdom, to the discovery of what life is really all about. For a man, the greatest block to his growth in wisdom is given in the next verse.

"*And I discovered more bitter than death the woman whose heart is snares and nets, whose hands are chains. One who is pleasing to God will escape from her, but the sinner will be captured by her*" *(Eccl. 7:26)*. Solomon speaks of a type of woman whose personality is dominated by her instinct to snare men like prisoners. In his Proverbs he advises: "My son, pay attention to my wisdom, listen well to my words of insight, that you may maintain discretion and your lips may preserve knowledge. For the lips of an adulteress drip honey, and her speech is smoother than oil; but in the end she is bitter as gall, sharp as a double-edged sword. Her feet go down to death; her steps lead straight to the grave" (Prov. 5:1-5 (*NIV*). What does this have to do with my problem? Seduction by a woman has everything to do with exposing a man's true character.

The problem began in the Garden of Eden (Gen. 3:6). Paul said that the man was not deceived like the woman, he knew exactly what he was doing; he wanted the woman more than he wanted God (1 Tim. 2:14). After the Fall, women would seek to control men through seduction (Gen. 3:16). Solomon speaks of the dark side of women and how it is used to control and manipulate men. I regularly hear complaints about the degrading way the media portrays human beings. However, are they degrading us or are they simply exposing our corruption? Solomon had experienced this control over his life (1 Kings 11:1-4; Neh. 13:26). Was Solomon bitter toward all women? Was he just a misogynist, as some say? In Ecclesiastes 9:9 he says, *"Enjoy life with the woman whom you love all the days of your fleeting life."*

When a person is viewed as an object of pleasure, there can be no discovery of wisdom. We do not relate or learn from objects of mere sensation. The man who fears God wants to please God. It will be seen in his sexual behavior, he will escape the seduction. The man who lives to please himself will not. Because of the "sexual seduction" that has infiltrated our culture, many women sadly become desensitized to how their attire can manipulate men rather than reflecting their identities as princesses of God.

You may be wondering about now if Solomon is picking on women? He's a man, but the reality goes both ways. Sexual seduction brings out the sin problem in both sexes. The dark side of man is to rule over the woman and have her serve his needs (Gen. 3:16). I'm sure you ladies get tired of being harassed by men who always have a hidden agenda. Do you really want your mind rewired to view human beings only as objects to dominate? I want to see people as they were created in the image of God with the very dignity they have been given by their Creator.

"'Behold, I have discovered this,' says the Preacher, 'adding one thing to another to find an explanation, which I am still seeking but have not found. I have found one man among a thousand, but I have not found a woman among all these'" (Eccl. 7:27-28). He says that in his lifetime, it was rare to find a man who only wanted to please God with his life. Regarding his relationships with women, he never did find one. However, remember this is more of a commentary on the way *he approached* women rather than a commentary on women (Eccl. 2:8). God's design for relationships between the sexes is not centered on sex but on mutual respect and honor before God. We have the same problem, and it can easily be seen by our tendencies toward sexual seduction. So now, the solution to the problem.

Here's the Solution to Our Problem, 7:29

"Behold, I have found only this, that God made men upright, but they have sought out many devices" (Eccl. 7:29). Here's the conclusion. "I have found" that we don't have to be this way. We weren't created to be this way. In *the beginning* God created us to be "upright." We were not created as a race of mindless beings. Rather, we were given a capacity for choice. If there is a freedom of choice, it necessitates the ability to make the wrong choices. When Adam and Eve chose to rebel, they acquired the knowledge of good *and evil.* This entails that humanity's future choices would be mixed with foolishness and pain. Whereas, the first man may have started the problem, we have become inventive with it, creative in using each other for our personal pleasure. The solution of the problem is a choice we have to make (John 3:3, 7; Rom. 6:23; and 2 Cor. 5:16-21). When will we begin to recognize and celebrate the image of God we see in each other?

The "Secrets of Kohelet" reveal how to live life and to live it well. It begins with wisdom, and wisdom comes from fearing God. Fearing God means that the drive of my life is to please Him—in all things.

CHAPTER 18

A Wise Understanding of Authority
Ecclesiastes 8:1-9

—⟶⟶—

None of us really like being told what to do and, yet, a fact of life is that there is authority in our lives. If we are ever going to have any kind of balance in living, it's important that we understand authority. Most of us, left to ourselves, have an authority problem. The concept of submission counters every natural drive we have. Here, in Ecclesiastes 8, Solomon is going to walk us through the wisdom of responding to the authorities in our life. What about the authority of human government? Is it an authority at all? Let me share something with you.

"All about us the warning signs of this collapse are apparent. Communism with its method of madness is making a powerful and insidious attack upon our dismayed and shattered nation. It seeks to poison and disrupt in order to hurt us into an epoch of chaos. This negative, destroying spirit spared nothing of all that is highest and most valuable. Beginning with the family, it has undermined the very foundations of morality and faith and scoffs at culture and business, nation and fatherland, justice, and honor.

"The National Government will regard it as its first and foremost duty to revive in the nation the spirit of unity and cooperation. It will preserve and defend those basic principles on which our nation has been built. It regards Christianity as the foundation of our national morality, and the family as the basis of national life. Turbulent instincts must be replaced by a national discipline as the guiding principle of our national life. All those institutions which are the strongholds of the energy and vitality of our nation will be taken under the special care of the government."

Sounds pretty good, huh? Most of us could submit to a government like that! This speech was delivered on February 1, 1933, to the German people by their new Chancellor of the Reich, Adolf Hitler.

In 1945, shortly after the communists took control of Rumania, Richard Wurmbrand and his wife began their work with the repressed Rumanian people. They were arrested and imprisoned in 1948, and it wasn't until sixteen years later in 1964 that he was released after much persecution and torture. You can understand his feelings as he penned them in a letter:

"We not only have the aim of smuggling Bibles or relief to families of Christian prisoners in communist countries, but of the overthrow of communist dictatorships, as every free man in times past wished the overthrow of the Nazi dictatorship. They would never have thought that the Jews under Hitler had to respect the Nazi authority. Not even the Jewish Christians were meant to obey the foolish laws of a dictator who had the intention to gas and burn them. A regime which tortures men to death because they are Christians has to disappear. In communist countries there are no authorities. According to the Bible an authority is an institution which has to punish evil and to reward good. The contrary happens under communist dictatorship. The ruler there is not an authority but a counter-authority."[1]

These are words from strong inner convictions and passionate feelings. What does the Bible say about governing authority or "counter-authority?" To Titus, Paul says, "Remind them to be subject to rulers, to authorities, to be obedient, to be ready for every good deed" (Titus 3:1). Likewise, Peter teaches that Christians are to submit to governing authorities (1 Pet. 2:13-17).

Authority Has a Design, 8:1-6

"Who is like the wise man and who knows the interpretation of a matter? A man's wisdom illumines him and causes his stern face to beam" (Eccl. 8:1). No one has an edge on the man who has wisdom. He has the "interpretation," the right understanding of how things around him fit into the scheme of his life. We say he has his "perspective." You can even see the uniqueness of a wise man in his countenance. There is peace, joy, and a non-fearing presence about him that can be seen in his face. He's actually cheerful, which will cause him to stand out from the crowd. That perspective has changed his hard, stern look to one of restfulness and contentment, and it is manifested on his face!

"I say, 'Keep the command of the king because of the oath before God'" (Eccl. 8:2). Kohelet provides advice concerning our behavior with kings. Like a typical sage, he's giving practical advice to young students on how to stay out of hot water; this is wisdom. Literally, his counsel is, "Keep the mouth of the King!" Rightful authority is to be obeyed. (See Rom. 13:1-5; Jer. 27:12ff; 29:7.) Proverbs warns us about the wrath of a king, "The terror of a king is like the growling of a lion; he who provokes his anger forfeits his life" (Prov. 20:2, *ESV*). Some feel the "King" mentioned here is God himself who is to be obeyed, but the following context appears to be more focused on earthly authority, not heavenly.

What is this oath? It is an oath of allegiance. In the ancient Near East, it was common for an oath to be taken between the king and the people before God. (This is comparable to reciting the Pledge of Allegiance.) Governing authority is rightful authority designed by God (Rom. 13:1-7).

"Do not be in a hurry to leave him. Do not join in an evil matter, for he will do whatever he pleases" (Eccl. 8:3). Unless you were a queen, few people could walk out on a king and live to tell the story. To walk out of his presence was to cast off your allegiance and your loyalty. The point is, who rules whom: the king over the people or the people over the king? Some have referred to the government of the United States as "The Great Experiment." The government is of the people, by the people, and for the people; but the people give that authority of rule to the ones they put into office.

Do we throw off our loyalty every time we are disappointed? Solomon says, "Do not join in an evil matter," rebellion or insurrection. Do not take part in an attempt to overthrow it. Although authority may be abused, it is not necessarily our right to overthrow it. Within the context of this particular passage, Solomon is informing his students that when a disagreement arises with a king, the prudent thing to do is avoid a confrontation.

"Since the word of the king is authoritative, who will say to him, 'What are you doing?'"(Eccl. 8:4). The ruler makes his judgments based on what he thinks is right. When it is all said and done, the final decision is made; it is his, and it is to be obeyed. The king's word is authoritative, thus, it is fruitless, even potentially dangerous, to oppose his decisions. We do have a process before final decisions to give our input and disagreement, but when the decision becomes law, it is *the law*!

"He who keeps a royal command experiences no trouble, for a wise heart knows the proper time and procedure" (Eccl. 8:5). Those who obey the king avoid the king's wrath, but an unrighteous king is likely to implement unrighteous commands. However, when the design is perverted by

those in authority, this promise is nullified. That is when the greatest weapon we have must be implemented. (See 1 Timothy 2:1-2.) A wise heart, however, discerns the procedure for change.

The key is in the timing. Do we really believe that God is in charge? The Bible teaches that vengeance belongs to God. In addition to this, we learn in Proverbs that "the tongue of the wise uses knowledge rightly" (Prov. 15:2). A quiet submission to the powers of authority will result in a peaceful life that will also free us up for the rendering to God.

"For there is a proper time and procedure for every delight, though a man's trouble is heavy upon him" (Eccl. 8:6). The wise understand that there is a time and place for everything. Daniel says, "Let the name of God be blessed forever and ever, for wisdom and power belong to Him. It is He who changes the times and the epochs; He removes kings and establishes kings; He gives wisdom to wise men and knowledge to men of understanding" (2:20-21). A wise person will be able to make competent decisions even when his heart is heavy and troubled.

Be Wise to Authority's Limitations, 8:7-8

"If no one knows what will happen, who can tell him when it will happen?" (Eccl. 8:7). No one knows, not even the king, when the hammer of God's judgment is going to fall. God is patient but, eventually, even His patience ends, and He acts. However, many of those in authority will continue to abuse that authority, oblivious to the fact that their power is from God and that they are to be accountable to Him. Therefore, we should always approach life with an attitude of humility.

"No man has authority to restrain the wind with the wind, or authority over the day of death; and there is no discharge in the time of war, and evil will not deliver those who practice it" (Eccl. 8:8). This is why our allegiance must ultimately

always be to God. And this is why we need not fret when even a king abuses his power. For, as powerful as a king is, he lacks the power to restrain the wind. Likewise, earthly kings are mortal. They do not live forever. They are finite.

What are our expectations of authority? Regarding governments and authority, we often develop an unspoken "make my life better" mentality. However, no matter what our expectations are of our next boss or our President, the truth is that even the greatest of human authorities cannot necessarily make things perfect for us. Authority figures and rulers have some real limitations:

1. They cannot control the wind. Governors, for example, as powerful as they are, cannot command the wind to bring rain to a desert wildfire.
2. Prime Ministers are unable to extend your life. Nor do they have the ultimate power over your sickness, accident, or aging.
3. Even the highest officials at the United Nations cannot protect you from war.
4. Authority figures are unable to protect you from the consequences of your actions (Gal. 6:7). Like the rule of gravity, if you sow evil you will eventually reap evil. God is just, and the ruler cannot protect you from God.

Ruling authority is designed by God and is to be obeyed. But it still has its limitations and cannot become a god to you. If it did, it would be an abusive god. But what are we to do when authority figures abuse their authority?

Be Wise to Authority's Abuses, 8:9
"All this I have seen and applied my mind to every deed that has been done under the sun wherein a man has exercised authority over another man to his hurt" (Eccl. 8:9).

Here Solomon is speaking about the abuse of power.[2] There are many instances in the Bible of authority figures abusing power. Shadrach, Meshach, and Abednego (Dan. 3:16-18) found themselves in a furnace as a result of the abuse of power as did their friend Daniel who ended up in the lion's den (Dan. 6:10). The Apostles Peter and Paul would lose their lives under the despot Caesar Nero.

In 1644 Samuel Rutherford wrote *Lex Rex*. The concept was rather simplistic and yet, profound: The law is king and, if the king and the government disobey the law, they are to be disobeyed. And the law is founded on the law of God. Specifically, Rutherford said: "A power ethical, politic, or moral, to oppress, is not from God and is not a power, but a licentious deviation of a power and is no more from God, but from sinful nature and the old serpent, than a license to sin."

For Rutherford, tyranny is defined as ruling without the sanction of God; and he suggested that there are three courses of action when encountering a tyrant:

1. Defend yourself by protest (i.e., legal action).
2. If possible, flee.
3. If necessary, use force to defend yourself.

This is similar to the philosophy of Francis Schaeffer who in the *Christian Manifesto* said: "One should not employ force if he may save himself by flight; nor should one employ flight if he can save himself and defend himself by protest and the employment of constitutional means of redress."[3]

Proverbs 24:21-22 says, "My son, fear the Lord and the king; do not associate with those who are given to change, for their calamity will rise suddenly, and who knows the ruin that comes from both of them?" Most of us aren't really thinking about starting a revolution but, if or when there is a "clash of conscience," it must be thought out *before* the crisis.

Take some action:

1. Register to vote. Only 50 percent of Christians eligible to vote are registered. Of those registered, only 25 percent actually vote on election day. This means just 12.5 percent of eligible Christians actually take part in the placing of men and women in the positions of authority over us.
2. Submit and honor all ruling authority with an attitude of reverence for God's ordinance. Justin Martyr, who was persecuted and beheaded by Marcus Aurelius Antoninus, wrote this in a letter to the emperor: "Everywhere, we more readily than all men, endeavor to pay to those appointed by you, the taxes, both ordinary and extraordinary, as we have been taught by Jesus. We worship only God, but in other things we will gladly serve you, acknowledging you as Kings and rulers of men, and praying that, with your kingly power, you may be found to also sound judgment."
3. Speak out in protest against the abuses of our government and don't hesitate to expose injustice and oppression.

CHAPTER 19

When God Doesn't Make Sense
Ecclesiastes 8:10-17

—⟋⟍—

We have learned to live with enigmas. We are surrounded by unsolved mysteries. The fine turning of the orbits in our solar system; earth rotating every twenty-four hours as it orbits the sun with the moon rotating every twenty-eight days with twenty-eight orbits around the earth and, yet, we will never see the back side of the moon. We are located in the perfect spot within our Milky Way galaxy; If we were much closer to the nucleus, the radiation would be too intense.

Inner space is also full of mysteries. If an electron was increased to the size of an apple, and a human being increased in size to the same proportion, that person could hold the entire solar system in the palm of his hand and would have to use a magnifying glass in order to see it.

Generally, we seem to co-exist with enigmas and yet, ironically, when God does something mysterious that affects our lives we immediately begin to question His character (or even His existence). There are times when God doesn't make sense. Some of the things He does or doesn't do are mysteries. We want to reduce God into something that is more manageable, a predictable formula that we can make sense of so we can use Him for our purposes. But God doesn't fit into our box.

He is not a cosmic Santa Claus in the sky, existing to pamper us, nor is He a cosmic policeman to protect our property.

He is not what you wanted your parents to be, and He is not the heavenly errand boy who is at your beck and call.

He is not a God in a box.

He is frightfully unpredictable. At times there is no other word to describe Him except for the word "mysterious."

I've noticed that God doesn't always do things the way I would. When I expect the bad guys to get it, they don't. Then I look around, and it's the good guys who are getting it. It's as if the bad guys get what the good guys deserve and the good guys get what the bad guys deserve. His judgments can be down right confusing. Why doesn't he come down hard on the *wicked* people?

There Is a Delayed Judgment, 8:10-11

"So then, I have seen the wicked buried, those who used to go in and out from the holy place, and they are soon forgotten in the city where they did thus. This too is futility" (Eccl. 8:10).

Sound confusing? You're in good company; some commentators believe that this is the most difficult verse in the book. In ancient Israel, a burial was an honoring event. The absence of a burial was similar to having a curse placed upon you. ("He will be buried with a donkey's burial, dragged off and thrown out beyond the gates of Jerusalem" Jer. 22:19.) Thus, Solomon is troubled by the fact that he has observed the wicked receiving a hero's burial. By contrast, I am reminded of a widow who, after listening to adulation heaped upon her undeserving dead husband, asked her son to go up and see if it was actually his father in the coffin.

They come to and fro to the "the place of the holy." This would be either Jerusalem proper or the Temple. In other words, they were acting like they were holy people and getting away with it. Could this be like hypocrites in church? Some translations have the word "praised" here instead of "forgotten." This is because both words have two Hebrew letters that are alike; *Beth*—"praise" and *Kaph*—"forgotten." The flow of thought seems to support the "praise" translation because, here they are being treated as "godly," when in reality they were rats! But if the word is "forgotten," the reference could be to the genuinely good folks who are forgotten while this "rat" is being honored. The point is simply this: either way, it's not fair! Retribution seems to be falling on the good guy. This too is futility. Again we see the Hebrew word *hevel*—this just doesn't make sense.

"Because the sentence against an evil deed is not executed quickly, therefore the hearts of the sons of men among them are given fully to do evil" (Eccl. 8:11), or as *The Message* says it: "Because the sentence against evil deeds is too long in coming, people in general think they can get by with murder." We see it all around us. Doesn't God realize that delayed punishment encourages evil? If you don't get in trouble when you should, you're likely to think that you will always get away with evil. What's going to stop you?

You look around and see what people are getting away with, and it is easy to think that there is a moral indifference or at least some complacency with God. Where is God? If nothing or no one intervenes to check sinners, surely they will continually regress and become even more brazen and calloused. Potentially, all of their intentions will be directed towards evil. This is the dark side to God's "forbearance" (Ps. 10:3-11). In summary, Solomon makes a somewhat obvious deduction: *if there is no apparent retribution for evil, it will flourish.*

There Will Be a Resolution to It, 8:12-13

"Although a sinner does evil a hundred times and may lengthen his life, still I know that it will be well for those who fear God, who fear Him openly. But it will not be well for the evil man and he will not lengthen his days like a shadow, because he does not fear God"(Eccl. 8:12-13). Even though the sinner may indefinitely get away with evil ("hundreds of times"), Solomon remains convinced that the God-fearer gets the better deal in the long run. Even if the sinner grows to an old age in his sin, Solomon says there is something that is not a mystery to him, something he knows (*yada*). Without a doubt, in the grand scheme of God's plan, it will go well (*tov*), it will be good for those who fear God. But how can he be so sure when, by his own declarations, there seems to be no retribution for the wicked? Remember, this journal is about life "under the sun." In the afterlife, however, it will make sense and these mysteries will be solved (Eccl. 12:13, 14).

Remember what it means to "fear God"? It is a holy caution that comes from a realization of God's greatness and, consequently, a reverence for Him. In other words, the way to safety is to fear God! For it will not be good for the wicked in the afterlife. What is an "evil man?" *The man who does not fear God.* It is as simple and straightforward as that. His life is like a shadow as the sun goes down, a picture of something that has no substance, something that is not real.

The sentence has been declared, but God is slow in executing it. However, justice delayed is not justice denied. Because there is an afterlife, both the apparent non-retribution of the wicked and the blessings of the righteous can theologically co-exist. Although the unrighteous can flourish in the natural world of the here and now, they will not be able to do so in the afterlife.

Sometimes It's Confusing, 8:14

"There is futility which is done on the earth, that is, there are righteous men to whom it happens according to the deeds of the wicked. On the other hand, there are evil men to whom it happens according to the deeds of the righteous. I say that this too is futility" (Eccl. 8:14).

Good people get what bad people should get, and bad people get what good people should get. Retribution and reward appear to be reversed.[1] Those devoted to God receive reproof by means of a scourge and are so afflicted at times that, it is as though they were displeasing to God. Job asked the same question: "Why do the wicked live on, growing old and increasing in power? They see their children established around them, their offspring before their eyes. Their homes are safe and free from fear; the rod of God is not upon them" (Job 21:7-9 *NIV*). Solomon gives two practical suggestions in the following two verses.

Here's the Wise Resolution to It, 8:15-17

"So I commended pleasure, for there is nothing good for a man under the sun except to eat and to drink and to be merry, and this will stand by him in his toils throughout the days of his life which God has given him under the sun" (Eccl. 8:15). He doesn't try to unravel it all or solve completely the enigma but, rather, he recommends pleasure, gladness, and enjoyment. (He has given this advice before: Eccl. 2:24; 3:12, 22). "Eat, drink and be merry." Do the things you enjoy, and receive them from the hand of God. As you receive and enjoy things from the hand of God, you will know that this is not an unjust indifferent deity who loves to confuse you with senselessness and pain. Enjoy what your God has for you. This will stand by you all the days of your life. So don't waste your lifetime trying to solve all of the mysteries of God. Enjoy what you *do* have and enjoy what you *do* know.

"When I gave my heart to know wisdom and to see the task which has been done on the earth (even though one should never sleep day or night), and I saw every work of God, I concluded that man cannot discover the work which has been done under the sun. Even though man should seek laboriously, he will not discover; and though the wise man should say, 'I know,' he cannot discover" (Eccl. 8:16-17). Laboring over a matter doesn't guarantee finding an answer. To believe otherwise is to begin with a rash assumption that all problems can be solved by man's intellect. Simply because something doesn't make sense to us doesn't mean that it's senseless. Regarding God, we have to *apprehend* that which we cannot always *comprehend*. Don't wait to understand it all; accept it as life and as His plan.

Why is it that life sometimes seems harder for the believer? When I was young, my friend and I got into trouble at school; and whereas, I also got in trouble again at home, my friend didn't. His parents didn't care and didn't do a thing.

Whether it's terrorism, pornography, or the drug industry, it certainly seems that the wicked are prospering. But don't be distracted from fearing God, and don't wait to understand it all. *Apprehend* that which you cannot *comprehend* by accepting the fact that God is in control and that vengeance belongs to Him (Rom. 12:19). Accept the mystery that God sees all and that He has a plan.

Let me challenge you to add one more mystery to your mystery list. This mystery is you. The issue is wisdom. You have enjoyed the good things from God. You have not forgotten Him, and you have learned that He is good and wise. Therefore, we must also trust in the fact that God has a plan that makes sense *to Him.* Therefore, we can accept the bad. This makes us a mystery to those around us. Meanwhile, enjoy the good. Fear God, eat, drink, and be merry.

CHAPTER 20

When the Curtain Falls
Ecclesiastes 9:1-10

—ɯ—

The Bible describes death as "precious" (Ps. 116:15); how do most people think about death? The answer is that they don't think about it. It's a morbid subject. Rousseau said, "He who pretends to face death without fear is a liar." When officiating at funerals, I am intrigued by people who, while showing respect for the deceased, would rather be anywhere but there. Often, people will avoid looking me in the eye. In *Man Alive*[1], Michael Green says, "Death has replaced sex as the forbidden subject of conversation in polite society." To make the subject a little more palatable, we've developed a new vocabulary:

- Death is referred to as "passing" or "passing away."
- The corpse is known as the "deceased."
- Many mortuaries prefer the name "chapel of rest."
- Modern cemeteries prefer names such as "garden of repose."

These changes may psychologically help make the subject more palatable, but it still fails to alleviate life's greatest challenge—*life has ended.* Why is death such an avoided subject? Some of the world's best writers have made attempts at broaching the issue:

- Epicurus, who authored the Epicurean ("go for the gusto") philosophy that focused on the pursuit of pleasure, was most notable for the motto: "Eat, drink and be merry for tomorrow we die." However, he was also the one who said, "What men fear is not that death is annihilation, but that it is not!"
- William Butler Yeats makes the same point in his poem, which is simply entitled *Death.* "Nor dread nor hope attends a dying animal; but a man awaits his end dreading and hoping all."
- T. S. Eliot (*Murder in the Cathedral*): "Behind the face of death the judgment and behind the judgment the void more horrid than active shapes of hell; emptiness, absence, separation from God; the horror of the effortless journey to the empty land which is no land, only emptiness, absence, the void, where those who were men can no longer turn the mind to distraction, delusion, escape into dreams, pretense."

If death is so dreadful and yet inevitable, what can be done about it? What are you going to do about it? Solomon has some insight. In Ecclesiastes chapters 1 and 2, we learned that life is a gift from God to be enjoyed. Chapters 3-5 revealed that God has a plan for each one of us. In chapters 6-8, Solomon explained the "plan" with all its mysteries and apparent inequities. Now, as we enter the last section of the book (which really began in Ecclesiastes 8:16), he applies the plan by reminding us to not let the mysteries of life rob us of the joy of living out the plan. That is, we cannot allow the apparent inequities of life to rob us of our motivation to enjoy the life God has given us. As is his custom, Solomon gets right to the point.

There's an Enigma to Death, 9:1-6
"For I have taken all this to my heart and explain it that righteous men, wise men, and their deeds are in the hand of God. Man does not know whether it will be love or hatred; anything awaits him" (Eccl. 9:1).

The righteous and the wise can take comfort that their deeds are in the hands of God. This is comforting because there will be times when you may question whether God is treating you as righteous or unrighteous. No one can predict the circumstances of their lives "under the sun." We do not know what life has in store for us, whether it will be good or bad; anything can happen. Like Job, it may be confusing to wonder whether God is for you or against you. Solomon has already warned us that prosperity is not all its cracked up to be (chapter 6) and adversity is not always as bad as we make it out to be (chapter 7). We tend to associate God's favor and disfavor with the good or bad of our current circumstances and status in life.

Job's friends were sincere in their counsel. We are told, "When they lifted up their eyes at a distance, and did not recognize him, they raised their voices and wept. And each of them tore his robe and they threw dust over their heads toward the sky. Then they sat down on the ground with him for seven days and seven nights with no one speaking a word to him, for they saw that his pain was very great" (Job 2:12-13). However, because of Job's adversity they were convinced that he must have sinned grievously to earn such disfavor from God. But was that really the case?

It is true that, at times, we do suffer under God's discipline. According to Walt Kaiser, the Bible teaches at least five additional reasons for suffering:

1. Educational (Job 35:9-11; 36:15)
2. Doxological, i.e., for the glory of God, e.g., the blind man (John 9:1-3)
3. Probationary: God is long-suffering in bringing judgment (2 Pet. 3:9)
4. Revelation, e.g., Hosea and the unfaithfulness of his wife (Hosea 1:2)
5. Sacrificial, e.g., Jesus Christ for the good of others (John 3:16)[2]

Solomon teaches that there is one suffering that is common to all of us. *"It is the same for all. There is one fate for the righteous and for the wicked; for the good, for the clean and for the unclean; for the man who offers a sacrifice and for the one who does not sacrifice. As the good man is, so is the sinner; as the swearer is, so is the one who is afraid to swear" (Eccl. 9:2).* There is one event that awaits all of us—good or bad. Unlike a dentist appointment, it cannot be rescheduled. Unless Jesus returns first, the curtain is going to fall on you. There is nothing you can do about it. You may be wicked or good, moral or immoral, Christian or atheist, vegetarian or meat eater; we are all going to die. The righteous are not visibly favored by providence nor are the unrighteous visibly rebuked by divine providence. Death comes indiscriminately to all.

"This is the evil in all that is done under the sun, that there is one fate for all men. Furthermore, the hearts of the sons of men are full of evil and insanity is in their hearts throughout their lives. Afterwards they go to the dead" (Eccl. 9:3). In *The Message*, Eugene Peterson says "It's one fate for everybody—righteous and wicked, good people, bad people, the nice and the nasty, worshipers and non-worshipers, committed and uncommitted. I find this outrageous—the worst thing about living on this earth—that everyone's lumped together in one fate. Is it any wonder that so many

people are obsessed with evil? Is it any wonder that people go crazy right and left; Life leads to death. That's it."

Solomon is not taking a nihilistic shot at God. The "evil" is "under the sun," something on this earth, and in the *natural* world that is evil. This evil is the "one-fate death." Death has caused all of us pain. It was the death of his friend Lazarus that caused Jesus to weep (John 11:35). Solomon says this indiscriminate death appears to encourage wickedness. "Hearts" are filled with "evil" and "insanity." Evil often results in a madness that has no regard for any consequences. But, if we all die the same, what does it matter? Who cares what you do or don't do? Somewhat rhetorically, Solomon quotes an ancient proverb:

"For whoever is joined with all the living, there is hope; surely a live dog is better than a dead lion" (Eccl. 9:4). As lowly and despicable a creature as a dog[3] was considered in the ancient Near East, it was still better to be a living dog than to be a mighty and majestic, but dead, lion. Life is key to doing something about your pending death. How is that? Read on.

"For the living know they will die; but the dead do not know anything, nor have they any longer a reward, for their memory is forgotten" (Eccl. 9:5). Does this mean that at death we are officially "kaput?" Is that it? We get buried and become flower food? That would be a contradiction to what Solomon said in Ecclesiastes 3:17. His point here is that when our shelf life on planet earth ends, so does our opportunity for reward from labor.

"Indeed their love, their hate and their zeal have already perished, and they will no longer have a share in all that is done under the sun" (Eccl. 9:6). The dead no longer have a part to play in the natural world. It's like graduating from high school. Regardless of whether or not you made the best of those years, or regret not learning Spanish or trying out for the football team—you're done. Solomon is saying that

we only get one life to live. Therefore, it's imperative that we make the most of it.

And There's an Enjoyment to Life, 9:7-10

"Go then, eat your bread in happiness and drink your wine with a cheerful heart; for God has already approved your works. Let your clothes be white all the time, and let not oil be lacking on your head. Enjoy life with the woman whom you love all the days of your fleeting life which He has given to you under the sun; for this is your reward in life and in your toil in which you have labored under the sun" *(Eccl. 9:7-9).*[4] Some may respond to Solomon's themes by allowing grief to consume them, by letting life's unexplained mysteries depress them, or by living a life of anxiety due to the certainty of death. However, his counsel is to eat your food, drink your wine, wear nice clothes, go to spas, and enjoy your wife (you get the picture).

In Solomon's day, only royalty or the wealthy would wear their white garments everyday. Common people reserved them for important and festive occasions. White garments were pictures of joy and festivity. This was also the case for perfuming or anointing yourself with oils. He is not teaching an unrestrained, extravagant lifestyle, but he is teaching that we should enjoy what we have—now.

This passage reminds me of a friend of mine that had a vintage 1970 Ford Mustang "Mach 1" with less than nine thousand original miles on it. He kept it in perfect condition and only drove it on special occasions, maybe four or five times a year. He kept it in the garage and under a cover. After getting married and having a child, he sold it. Shortly thereafter, I began to see that car all the time. The new owner really seems to enjoy it. He constantly receives comments from fellow car enthusiasts, and he keeps it in great condition—but he drives it! Ironically, as much as my friend loved that Ford Mach 1, the new owner *enjoys* it.

There is also an interesting statement about marriage here. Celibacy is not a more sacred state than matrimony. The writer of Hebrews makes the same point in Hebrews 13:4 "Let marriage be held in honor among all, and let the marriage bed be undefiled." Marriage is God's design from the beginning (Gen. 2:24). Men should get married. The only biblical exceptions are:

1. When the gift of celibacy is given (1 Cor. 7:7).
2. During times of persecution when marriage would be an additional pressure rather than a joy (Jer. 16:1-4; 1 Cor. 7:26, 29).

He says "Enjoy life with the woman you love all the days of your fleeting life." The Hebrew word "enjoy" here is literally "see" by continually experiencing all of human emotions, passions and companionship. In other words, enjoy life with your wife by learning to enjoy her. Speaking of which…

"Whatever your hand finds to do, do it with all your might; for there is no activity or planning or knowledge or wisdom in Sheol where you are going" (Eccl. 9:10). In the New Testament, Paul takes it a step further: "Whatever you do, do your work heartily, as for the Lord rather than for men" (Col. 3:23). Here's the key. Now is the time to get on with it. Enjoy life by doing what is significant and important with your life. This is what Jesus was referring to in John 9:4, "We must work the works of him who sent me, as long as it is day; night is coming when no man can work." It is on this side of the grave that we must do the significant for God—and the time is now, for when death comes the days of opportunity will have passed. So, in whatever stage of life you are—newlywed or aging citizen—be all that you can be by enjoying all you can do.

The grief you endure, the mysteries of the presence of evil, the common fate of death for all—let none of these be obstacles to dedicating yourself to the significant work of God. It comes down to being devoted. Interesting enough, our word "devotion" comes from two little words *de* (from) and *vovere* (to vow) or to dedicate yourself by a vow.

1. Be devoted to life. Learn that God is good by enjoying the good he's given you. Then you will be able to trust Him for the mysterious bad.
2. Be devoted to the Author of Life. You have one shot at life, one life to get this right. Begin now to make the most of it (Hebrews 9:27-28).

CHAPTER 21

Success to the Unsuspecting
Ecclesiastes 9:11-18

—ɯ—

I have never met anyone who enjoys losing or being disappointed. Who likes to fail? We all have a desire to be successful in what we set our minds to do. Because of our desire to succeed, we create formulas that are designed to assist us in this quest. These formulas usually contain the following:

1. Seize the opportunities for advancement and be swift to take advantage of them.
2. Work long and hard. A healthy competitive spirit will take you a long way.
3. Work smart. Good sense is a necessity for being successful.
4. Demonstrate shrewdness and meticulous attention to what is in front of you.
5. Knowledge is power. If you want to get to the top, you must prepare yourself with education and training.

However, here is the million dollar question: Can success be reduced to a predictable formula that can be followed like a map of Disneyland, leading you every time to Fantasyland?

There are two Olympic sports that I greatly admire and yet, simultaneously, can barely endure to watch—ice skating and gymnastics. I remember watching gymnast Debbie Thomas being penalized half a point for falling, which resulted in the Americans being eliminated from the medal ceremonies by the East Germans. After all that work and discipline, she didn't make it.

Was it bad luck or just a bad break? Is the element of luck the great neutralizer in the formula for being successful? Have you ever tried everything, including prayer, and something still failed? Think of your last disappointment. How long did it take you to get over it? The following eight verses have something to teach us about success (and formulas for success) and luck. He begins with...

There's a Failing Formula, 9:11-12

"I again saw under the sun that the race is not to the swift and the battle is not to the warriors, and neither is bread to the wise nor wealth to the discerning nor favor to men of ability; for time and chance overtake them all" (Eccl. 9:11). The Hebrew text here in verse 11 has five negatives, and each begins the five different phrases. Literally, the verse would read, "Not to the swift is the race; not to the warriors is the battle; not to the wise is the bread; not to the discerning is the wealth; not to the men of ability is the favor." In other words, the path to success is not always the way we think. These five words and these five assets appear to be everything you would need to guarantee success.

1. The swift: we would say they are quick to see and to grab the opportunities.

2. The warrior or strong: we would say they are tough and competitive.
3. The wise: we would say they are the ones with good sense.
4. The discerning: we would say they are shrewd and meticulous.
5. The able: we would say they are the educated and trained.

Simply put, human abilities do not *guarantee* success. As the former tennis pro John McEnroe once said, "I'd rather be lucky than good." Ultimately, success or failure does not depend entirely on our effort, but also upon the effort of something else. Luck. What is luck? Is there such a thing as luck in the Christian's life? Doesn't God cause it all to happen or not happen? Is God in control of this? Did forces of darkness intervene? I have always said that luck is simply when opportunity meets ability. The latter, you control and the former, you don't. By definition, luck means "to prosper or succeed through chance or good fortune." To be lucky is to produce or get a result by chance.

Time. There is an occasion and opportunity for things to happen. However, that time is not always predictable nor is it bound to our formula for success. The use of the word "chance" suggests an occurrence (i.e. something happens). For example, in Ruth, we read that "[Ruth] *happened* to come to the portion of field belonging to Boaz, who was of the family of Elimelech" (Ruth 2:3). Some translators actually translate it "she happened upon her chance." Both words are two different forms of the same root; literally "her chance" (noun), "chanced" (verb).

There is a similar concept expressed regarding David's entry into Saul's court. Shortly after God removed His anointing from Saul, Saul began to experience despondent, jealous, and violent behavior. Saul's servants suggested music, specifically a harpist, as a remedy. "Then one of the young men said, 'Behold, I have seen a son of Jesse the Bethlehemite who is a skillful musician'" (1 Sam. 16:18a, *NASB*). As a result, David is brought into contact with Saul and the rest is history.

God permits events to happen, yet He is more interested in our responses to them than He is in the event itself. He knows He can take any event that occurs and still produce good out of it. The issue is, when you fall down, what do you fall back on? God's power is in the results and the control:

Providence: The care or benevolent guidance of God
Provident: Making provision for the future
Providential: Marked by foresight; (synonym-lucky)

Time and chance are paired because they both have a way of suddenly taking matters out of our hands.

"Moreover, man does not know his time: like fish caught in a treacherous net and birds trapped in a snare, so the sons of men are ensnared at an evil time when it suddenly falls on them" (Eccl. 9:12). These two similes of the "fish" and "birds" are aimed to stress how unexpectedly things can happen. Neither of the creatures ever anticipated their predicaments. Likewise, we do not always know our time or chance. Much of life feels out of our control. Our lives are in the hands of God, and we can never be certain of what life will look like by the end of the day. For the believer, *luck* or *chance* is simply God's providence in taking the combination of your work and preparation, along with life's events, and blending them together for His purposes (Jas. 4:15-16). We cannot control or manipulate it. There is a point where we must take a serious look at His sovereign providential care because that is the fruitful plan.

There's a Fruitful Plan, 9:13-18

Solomon gives us a parable to help make a critical point to this whole discussion. *"Also this I came to see as wisdom under the sun, and it impressed me. There was a small city with few men in it and a great king came to it, surrounded it and constructed large siege works against it. But there was found in it a poor wise man and he delivered the city by his wisdom, yet no one remembered that poor man"* (Eccl. 9:13-15).

Because it's a parable, we cannot be certain if this is actually an account of a real siege. However, it is possible that Solomon may have been told or that he remembered an event in his life. A king comes upon a small city and builds large embankments or mounds raised high enough to go over the walls and into the town.[1] Due to the fact that it's no ordinary king but a *great* king, and not just an ordinary siege but a *large* seige, it would appear that the city had no chance, yet it is saved by the wisdom of a *poor* man. We are not told what he did. With his wisdom he saves the day, and the poor guy gets nothing for it. His ungrateful countrymen forgot his very existence. You would have expected the guy to be able to retire on his accolades or that a statue would be erected in his honor; but no—nothing. Even his name was forgotten.

Here's the question—*was he successful?*

Perhaps you can relate. Maybe someone "stole" your idea or perhaps someone received credit for your work. Wisdom is that gift that comes from fearing God, from that passion to please Him. It means doing the right thing whether or not you will receive accolades for it. We please Him by doing what is right, but doing what is not always popular or rewarded. Wisdom is not always rewarded with success in this life.

"So I said, 'Wisdom is better than strength.' But the wisdom of the poor man is despised and his words are not heeded. The words of the wise heard in quietness are better than the shouting of a ruler among fools. Wisdom is better

than weapons of war, but one sinner destroys much good" *(Eccl. 9-16-18).* A better rendering is "the wise words are heard in quiet and are better than the shouts of a chief among fools." In other words, we tend to be more impressed with the position of the man than the content of what he is saying; thus, unknowingly, we can let him destroy us with his foolish counsel. In spite of wisdom's power, generally, people tend to disregard it if it's spoken by a poor man. By contrast, a person's prominence makes him more likely to be heard. Regardless, words of wisdom are more effective than weapons because weapons can only change behavior, whereas wisdom can change the heart. Real success is the touching of lives for good. If we are ever going to grow in wisdom, we must learn to prepare for and respond to disappointment.

1. When I've done everything I can do, followed every formula for succeeding, and it still doesn't happen, what do I do?
2. When I get my act together and, because of some chance deal, it vaporizes in my face, what do I do?
3. When I have prepared a lifetime for something and, right when I'm ready to enjoy it, my health goes, what do I do?

Human ability cannot guarantee success and yet, wisdom tells us to prepare well for it. Be swift, strong, wise, discerning and able; but remember: "God's sovereign, providential care" takes the combination of your work and preparation, combined with life's good or bad occurrences, and blends them together into His responsibility. "In his heart a man plans his course, but the Lord determines his steps" (Prov. 16:9).

CHAPTER 22

The Art of Good Sense, Part 1
Ecclesiastes 10:1-11

—⟋⟍—

The old Dutch proverb says, "Vee grow too soon oldt, and too late smart." With life comes aging, and with aging comes wisdom; but it seems that by the time we've learned life's lessons, it is too late to apply them. We have already learned from Solomon that life doesn't always make sense—it's vaporous. Therefore, exceptionally good sense is needed.

Typically, it's easy to point out the frustrations and problems of life, but there's a management maxim that says: "Don't bring me problems, bring me solutions." Solomon doesn't spend much time on the problems, but rather upon the practical solutions, something that will help bring some sense to it all. Solomon proceeds to provide some good biblical sense. He begins with some good sense about your reputation.

What About Your Reputation? 10:1-3
What is reputation? The quickest answer is that it is what people think of when they think of you. Obviously, we all desire that people think the best of us...all the time. But here

"under the sun," our name and reputation are as fragile as a crystal glass sitting at the edge of the table.

"Dead flies make a perfumer's oil stink, so a little foolishness is weightier than wisdom and honor" (Eccl. 10:1). It doesn't take much to ruin a good name. We can make all kinds of mistakes; but those "reputation mistakes" will actually damage your name. It's like buying some precious perfume and finding a dead fly in it. The point is that something as little as a dead insect can ruin the whole bottle. This is a painful and sobering fact: it only takes one foolish act to impair credibility in the eyes of others. Whether it's Barry Bonds, Pete Rose, Monica Lewinsky, or an entire corporation like Enron, one indiscretion can overshadow a lifetime of achievements. I have always said that a reputation is built on sweating the small things. What are these "reputation mistakes?"

"A wise man's heart directs him toward the right, but the foolish man's heart directs him toward the left" (Eccl. 10:2). In Solomon's culture, the "right" spoke of the place of honor. Whereas, no offense to you lefties, the left spoke of dishonor and disfavor. Our actions reveal our heart. Jesus said, "Where a man's treasure is there his heart is also" (Matt. 6:21). In Proverbs 4:23, you are instructed to "watch over your heart with all diligence, for from it flows the springs of life." The Hebrew word for heart is *lev* and the Greek is *kardia*. Both are used throughout the Bible in reference to the inner man: our thinking, inclinations, resolutions, will, affections, passions, and our moral character. It's where the real you begins. "Jesus said, "That which proceeds out of the man, that is what defiles the man. For from within, out of the heart of men, proceed the evil thoughts, fornications, thefts, murders, adulteries, deeds of coveting and wickedness, as well as deceit, sensuality, envy, slander, pride, and foolishness. All these things proceed from within and defile the man" (Mark 7:20-23).

God, of course, has the ability to transform hearts, thus altering our innermost being (2 Cor. 5:17). Likewise, the Bible tells us that we can harden our hearts by refusing to allow God to change us.

"*Even when the fool walks along the road, his sense is lacking and he demonstrates to everyone that he is a fool*" *(Eccl. 10:3)*. Lewis Sperry Chafer said, "It is much better to keep silent and let everybody think you are a fool, than to open your mouth and remove all doubt." Even when a foolish man does what is right, he is still foolish because he doesn't know why it is right. Even a broken clock is correct twice a day. It's like the man who jumps into the sea to save a drowning man. When asked why he did it, his response was "I had to, he was wearing my watch" (i.e. the right action for the wrong reason). This type of person has a hardened heart. He will never understand life, and he will continually make immoral and unwise choices.

Solomon is giving a warning to his students. If you think in terms of what you can get away with, you are already in trouble. We need to proactively fight for our character. But how?

What About Your Composure? 10:4-7

"*If the ruler's temper rises against you, do not abandon your position, because composure allays great offenses*"(*Eccl. 10:4*). Here is a picture of a counselor giving some advice to a king. Instead of being grateful for it, the king gets mad. If someone with authority over you becomes angry with you, what do you do? Specifically, what is the wise counsel of action when your boss (or someone in authority) is irate with you? Should you become a "yes man"? Solomon teaches that you should not abandon your position (or post). In other words, don't resign or run from the situation. Exercise your composure so that calmness and self-control are translated into a "yielding." A calm, conciliatory spirit goes a long way and earns respect. Discretion is a virtue. Choose your battles wisely. Composure and a yielding spirit are great assets. We are told that "a soft answer turns away wrath" (Prov. 15:1). Composure says something about you and your heart. Additionally, it is the wisest course of action when a superior is angry with you.

"There is an evil I have seen under the sun, like an error which goes forth from the ruler" (Eccl. 10:5). Solomon says that something is not right "under the sun," and it is an error in judgment on the part of unwise rulers. They put the wrong people in positions of authority!

"Folly is set in many exalted places while rich men sit in humble places" (Eccl. 10:6). By "rich," he is not referring to their money but rather to their nobility. It is those who would not be motivated to seek office for financial gain. People *without* the credentials are provided the opportunity, whereas those without the opportunity are the ones with the ability. The evil (10:5) in this is the result of negligent error where there can be great repercussions for many.[1]

"I have seen slaves riding on horses and princes walking like slaves on the land" (Eccl. 10:7). Ironically, Solomon is saying that the wrong men are on the horses. As a result of inept leadership (v. 6) society is in chaos. Basically, wisdom benefits society, but foolishness damages it. The wise are appointed to low positions, and the fools are in positions of influence and leadership. This is maddening. These are the repercussions of fools in leadership (v.6).

Warnings About Success, 10:8-11

"He who digs a pit may fall into it, and a serpent may bite him who breaks through a wall" (Eccl. 10:8). I don't know about you, but the preceding section was a little on the depressing side for me. However, we must remember that Ecclesiastes is one of the rawest books in Scripture. It candidly reveals how life is and not how it should be; and

yet, as the saying goes: "We're not out of the woods yet." We still need some counsel in navigating through life. Solomon proceeds to teach his students five short proverbs, which he groups into two pairs with one summary.

First, there are two forms of destructive behavior. A pit was dug in order to capture... wild animals? An enemy? We cannot know with absolute certainty, but we do know that the instrument used to capture someone may be the very thing that captures *you*. This verse was a popular saying in Ancient Wisdom literature.[2] In the United States, we have our own proverb for this which goes something like: "That one may come back to bite you." Furthermore, the verse can imply that we should use caution in our routine activities. Don't become careless due to familiarity.

While breaking down a wall, you may well come across a snake. When you go about making changes, be aware of the dangers. Breaking down a person's resistance can come back to bite you as well. Things don't always change that easily. These accidents (digging a pit and breaking down a wall), while routine, possess the potential to bring us harm. Basically, you can never be too careful.

"He who quarries stones may be hurt by them, and he who splits logs may be endangered by them" (Eccl. 10:9). Here we are presented with two forms of constructive labor, both with occupational hazards. While I have never quarried, I have done some lumberjacking. Perhaps even you corporate types have experienced a Norman Rockwell moment by cutting down your very own Christmas tree. How romantic. Not! You can get stuck in the mud...you can cut yourself with the saw...splinters...you can get into an argument with your spouse about which tree to cut down...the tree can fall on you. Why does everything have to be so hard and what is the point? The point is that we need to be cognizant of Murphy's Law (i.e., if it can go wrong it will). Life can

be hazardous. Be careful. Solomon summarizes this in the following proverb:

"If the axe is dull and he does not sharpen its edge, then he must exert more strength. Wisdom has the advantage of giving success" (Eccl. 10:10). I remember hearing my mother say, "An ounce of prevention is worth a pound of cure," and "Haste makes waste," etc. As it turns out, she was right. When you don't sharpen the axe, the job becomes more difficult. A dull axe may result in injury or accident due to the additional force that is needed to wield it. While it may appear that preparation is slowing things down, the truth is, it will speed and enhance the process once initiated. "Wisdom has the advantage of giving success" because wisdom prevents "reputation mistakes."

"If the serpent bites before being charmed, there is no profit for the charmer" (Eccl. 10:11). Although the profession of snake charmer has fallen on hard times, in Solomon's day it was a culturally acceptable way to make a living. This business (snake charming) possessed one very practical consideration: if the snake bites the charmer before he has had a chance to charm it, he is too late. The damage has been done. Once he is bitten, you won't be getting much of his services. Don't wait until it is too late to apply wisdom.

"Folly" is a term that has fallen out of use in contemporary English, but it is a term used rather frequently in the Scriptures. It basically means, the lack of foresight, failing to realize the consequences of action before they occur (2 Peter 10-11). Remember, wisdom is making the connections between decisions and consequences. There are inherent dangers in just about everything we do. This doesn't mean that we are to live timid lives of fear. Simply look both ways before you cross the streets of life. Use your abilities wisely.

CHAPTER 23

The Art of Good Sense, Part 2
Ecclesiastes 10:12-20

—ɯ—

When life doesn't make sense, you must make sure that at least what you do makes sense. Otherwise, senselessness is matched with senselessness, and that isn't going to make sense out of anything. (You may want to read that again.) When you are talking to a doctor about something that is serious, you don't want him trying to ease your mind with platitudes; but rather you need the painful truth and you need it straight. Dr. Solomon cuts it sharp and clean. In the previous chapter, we were introduced to "reputation mistakes." Now Solomon shows us the things that potentially cause irreparable damage to our influence on others. He takes us to the arena of our mouths, our thinking, and our judgment.

What About Our Big Mouths? 10:12-14
"Words from the mouth of a wise man are gracious, while the lips of a fool consume him" (Eccl. 10:12). To an ancient reader (or hearer), the transition from verse 11 to 12 is quite witty. In verse 11, "charmer" can also be translated as "master of the tongue."[1] Your mouth is a direct link to your wisdom because it is a direct expression of your heart. This

is the acid test of wisdom (Matt. 12:33-37). In the previous section, we learned that the "heart" is the intimate you—the real you—and your deep inclinations. Your thoughts and desires will not stay hidden because your mouth will betray the confidence. Here he says that the words of a wise man are literally "grace." This has two possible meanings. He speaks of the fact that words are either the means by which grace is given or by which grace is received. Either way, words are the pegs on which thoughts hang. My mouth will either cause me to give grace or to receive grace. How?

1. To give grace: This is achieved by expressing truth correctly to one another; the truth of another's worth and of the plan God has for them; the truth of hope because of God's plan. The power of the tongue is mentioned throughout Proverbs (15:1-4; 22:11; 25:15). The very words Jesus used were described in Luke 4:22, "And all were speaking well of Him, and wondering at the gracious words which were falling from His lips." The Apostle Paul warns us in Ephesians 4:29-30 that once something is said it cannot be unsaid. The damage is done. The snake has bitten. (See Jas. 4:15-16.)

2. To receive grace: Favor is found by seeking counsel.
   - Proverbs 13:10: "With those who receive counsel is wisdom."
   - Proverbs 19:20 "Listen to counsel and accept discipline that you may be wise the rest of your days;"
   - Proverbs 25:12 "Like an earring of God and an ornament of fine gold is a wise reprover to a listening ear."

But of the foolish, Proverbs 18:2 says, "[He] delights only in revealing his own mind." To go out and do something tragic and *then* seek counsel is too late. The mouth of a foolish person will "consume him." He will swallow himself up in self-destruction.

"The beginning of his talking is folly and the end of it is wicked madness" (Eccl. 10:13). The foolish begins with the wrong premise; thus, no matter how logically he thinks, he may end in "madness." In other words, he will talk himself into confusion and moral perversity. He is unaware that there is a "time for silence" (Eccl. 3:7).

"Yet the fool multiplies words. No man knows what will happen, and who can tell him what will come after him?" (Eccl. 10:14). "Fools talk way too much, chattering stuff they know nothing about" (Eccl. 10:14, *The Message*). I once overheard a conversation about a friend who always talked about the same thing. When asked, "What does he talk about?" The answer was, "I don't know, he really never says." Why would one use so many words to say so little? Many words are used to convince not only others but yourself of what you are not sure. The fool speaks as if he knows everything, even the future (what will come after him). By contrast, in Proverbs we are told, "Do not boast about tomorrow, for you do not know what a day may bring forth. Let another praise you, and not your own mouth; a stranger, and not your own lips" (Prov. 27:1-2). Using our mouths wisely means that we are either giving grace to others or receiving it.

About our words, James warned: "So also the tongue is a small part of the body, and yet it boasts of great things. See how great a forest is set aflame by such a small fire. And the tongue is a fire" (Jas. 3:5-6a).

What About Good Thinking? 10:15-17

"The toil of a fool so wearies him that he does not even know how to go to a city" (Eccl. 10:15). The fool works hard but not smart. "Not knowing the way to a city" is a prover-

bial saying for not understanding the most obvious of things. Folly has nothing to do with IQ. As Shakespeare's Macbeth said, "A tale told by an idiot full of sound and fury is signifying nothing." Because he's all talk and believes he knows everything; he knows nothing about the most obvious of things. The issue is how teachable are you? In other words, how responsible is your thinking?

"Woe to you, O land, whose king is a lad and whose princes feast in the morning. Blessed are you, O land, whose king is of nobility and whose princes eat at the appropriate time—for strength and not for drunkenness" (Eccl. 10:16-17). This is actually a dirge (a mournful song used at funerals), and its usage here is very befitting. The reference to a child has less to do with age and more with maturity. An irresponsible or inept ruler equals trouble for everyone under his authority. It appears that partying and opulent living had become normal for them and that they began their days with play rather than work. They were consumed with feasting and partying instead of prioritizing the responsibilities of the state. But one who does understand, the "King of nobility," knows the time to carry out responsibility with "appropriate time" for play.

I like the way Michael Eaton put it in his commentary on this text: "Drinking in the early hours of the day marked a dissolute, slothful approach to life, with emphasis on luxury and personal indulgence. As we have frequently seen, personal enjoyment had a place. The antithesis to indulgence here is not asceticism, but self-control. The mark of such pleasure is that it is to be enjoyed 'in a state of strength,' not 'in a state of drunkenness.'"[2]

Wisdom (nobility) understands and prioritizes responsibility. Irresponsibility is the life of a foolish child. When I was child, I spoke and did as a child, but now...do you understand your responsibilities? Don't wait until the snake has already bitten. However, before moving on, we must understand how to use wisdom in the area of...

And What About Good Judgment? *10:18-20*
"Through indolence the rafters sag, and through slackness the house leaks. Men prepare a meal for enjoyment, and wine makes life merry, and money is the answer to everything" (Eccl. 10:18-19). "Indolence" and "slackness" indicate sluggishness, idleness, laziness, and the dislike of work. The flat roofs of Eastern houses demanded continual attention. Many were covered with lime. Like plaster, because of their exposure to the elements, they required regular maintenance. Sagging supports and leaky roofs were proverbial phrases for not attending to business and for making poor choices.

In principle, banqueting is a perfectly acceptable activity, but it is something that can easily be mismanaged by the unwise. For the foolish, life is merely an amusement, and they don't see the big picture. The words of the careless are: "For laughter they make bread, and it is wine that gladdens life, and it is money that is the answer to everything."

This reflects the worldview of the unwise. Food, wine, and money are the limits of their horizon.

"Furthermore, in your bedchamber do not curse a king, and in your sleeping rooms do not curse a rich man, for a bird of the heavens will carry the sound and the winged creature will make the matter known" (Eccl. 10:20). This is yet another proverb that has worked its way into our contemporary vocabulary via the expression: "A little bird told me." Be careful what you say about your boss or any prominent and influential person. While you may be assured that everything will be kept confidential; somehow the cat has a way of getting out of the bag, doesn't it? And once spoken—well, we all know how hard it is to get that cat back into the bag. Therefore, as our parents taught us: if you can't say something nice, its best to say nothing at all. When it is about your

boss or an influential person, you must take extra precautions. Once again, it is a question of judgment!

Remember the snake. Don't wait until it has bitten, for once the snake has bitten it is too late. Wisdom is using good sense before it is too late when it comes to my mouth, my thinking and my judgment.

CHAPTER 24

Casting Bread upon the Waters
Ecclesiastes 11:1-6

—⟋⟍—

W e have all been asked at one time to give to a worthy cause. First, we want to determine if it actually *is* a worthy cause but then, can we find a reason *not* to give? Why is generosity such an obstacle for so many of us? Granted, we need to be cautious to avoid being conned or scammed. Yet, for many it is simply the result of selfishness and fear. This is probably why so many people are uneasy discussing the subject of giving and money.

Most of us work towards a certain quality of life, and giving anything away seems to defeat the purpose. C. S. Lewis said, "For many of us the obstacle to charity lies not in our luxurious living or desire for more money, but in our fear—fear of insecurity."[1] Solomon offers sound advice when it comes to generosity, and he does it by contrasting three analogies.

The Wisdom of Investing Instead of Hoarding 11:1-2

"Cast your bread on the surface of the waters, for you will find it after many days" (Eccl. 11:1). Waterlogged bread doesn't sound very appetizing, but that would be missing the

point. Bread in the ancient Near East was made in the form of thin cakes, which would actually float for a time if thrown onto water. But who would fling bread into the water? There is an Aramaic Proverb of Ben Sira that says, "Scatter thy bread on the water and on the dry land; in the end of the days thou findest it again." A similar Arabic Proverb says, "Do good, cast they bread into the water, thou shalt be repaid some day." Some commentators believe this is a reference to foreign investments with ships on commercial voyages that might be delayed before any profit resulted. Indeed, one interpretation might be that Solomon is encouraging his students to invest abroad. However, based on the context, it seems more likely that, although the figure of speech may have originated from the realm of commerce, Solomon is talking about a different type of investment. *Giving.*

We must be open to the realm of charitable giving without thought of personal gain. What may seem like a waste for some may be the best "investment" ever made. God says, I'll give you a chance to trust a promise. Cast your bread upon the waters, give of your wealth to those who have need, and understand the promise of Proverbs 19:17: "One who is gracious to a poor man lends to the Lord, and he will repay him for his good deed."

"Divide your portion to seven, or even to eight, for you do not know what misfortune may occur on the earth" (Eccl. 11:2). Again Solomon warns us about the uncertainties of life. To carry the idiom from the preceding verse further, if one ship is destroyed in a storm or its cargo stolen, other vessels would return to you. That is, don't put all your eggs in one basket. However, like the preceding verse, this particular phrase "Divide your portion to seven, or even to eight," is a Hebrew way of saying, "Be generous to as many as you can and then some." Specifically, a time may come when you will need a little help from your friends. This carries

the same connotation as "be nice to people on the way up because you may need them on the way down."

The Wisdom of Making a Decision Instead of Not, 11:3-4

"If the clouds are full, they pour out rain upon the earth; and whether a tree falls toward the south or toward the north, wherever the tree falls, there it lies" (Eccl. 11:3). There is a contrast between these two and yet, they share one thing in common. Approaching storm clouds bringing torrential rain can be watched with apprehension as they come. A tree falling, whether to the south or to the north, is sudden and could never have been anticipated. And yet, we have control over neither.

There are some things in life that we dread. Likewise, there are other dreadful things awaiting us in the future that we cannot anticipate. Regardless, there are things we cannot control. While we need to be prudent and prepare for the unexpected, these uncertainties should not be allowed to paralyze us in our generosity. I know what some of you are thinking: "I'm just not sure that I'm in a position to be generous right now. Things can always take a turn for the worse, and so I had better play it safe. When things get better I will be generous. God understands." You are right. This is one of the ancient secrets of Kohelet. Things may take a turn for the worse. Solomon concurs that life is uncertain. However, you cannot sit back and wait until everything is secure before you invest your life into the life of others. Because of life's uncertainties, the time to invest is now. For example…

"He who watches the wind will not sow and he who looks at the clouds will not reap" (Eccl. 11:4). Those who insist on certainties or favorable conditions before investing in the lives of others will never do anything. If a farmer waits too long for ideal weather conditions to plant, he may subsequently miss the opportunity to harvest. Forethought and timely action are important, but we must avoid analysis

paralysis. There is an element of risk here. We speak of high risk, high profit and low risk, low profit but either way risk is present. It's easy to believe in our minds that God keeps His promises, but can we really believe in our hearts that He does? Compounding this is the pressure to distinguish between honest risk and foolish stewardship? What is going to motivate me to be generous?

The Wisdom of Trusting Instead of Doubting, 11:5-6

"Just as you do not know the path of the wind and how bones are formed in the womb of the pregnant woman, so you do not know the activity of God who makes all things" (Eccl. 11:5).

There are things about the wind that we do not understand nor can we predict. Like the wind, there are complexities of life still very much a mystery. The Midrash[2] recognizes physical conception as one of the seven great mysteries of God. However, the analogy illustrates our need to focus on what we know, rather than the certainty our future. As discussed earlier (and in 11:2), there are mysteries of life that we will never fully comprehend; and yet, we do not wait for complete knowledge before we trust and obey. As with the wind and pregnancy, we can see God's activity in the world, but our minds cannot completely apprehend it all. Therefore, we must apprehend the "truths" we *do* understand and trust Him for what we *do not*. Twice in verse 5 and 6 you find the phrase, "You do not know." But the key phrase here is in verse 6.

"Sow your seed in the morning and do not be idle in the evening, for you do not know whether morning or evening sowing will succeed, or whether both of them alike will be good" Eccl. 11:6). Here Solomon draws his conclusion. The key phrase is "do not be idle," or as it is translated in the King James Version, "withhold not thine hand." Let the results, be it success or failure, rest in the hand of God. But do not just

sit there waiting for secure guarantees for life. Do something now, right where you are.

"In the morning and in the evening" speak volumes about making each day count. If it is the morning or the evening which may speak of aging, let your life count. If it is the whole day, let your life count by counting for someone else. This is a warning against discouragement! Encouragement comes from realizing that our lives are overseen by God. In the words of the writer of Hebrews, "For God is not unjust so as to forget your work and the love which you have shown toward His name, in having ministered and in still ministering to the saints" (Heb. 6:10). A life of faith does not remove the problem of our ignorance, but rather enables us to embrace it. So with this issue of generosity, can you trust God as the Great Equalizer?

"So you do not know the activity of God who makes all things." This phrase (in 11:5) summarizes Solomon's conclusion. No one can fully know or understand God's plans. What are we to do? *We are to act on what He has revealed to us.* There are many works and results that God brings to pass even out of our humble efforts at being generous, even when the odds seemed strongly against any success. Our inability to see how our giving can make any significant difference should never deter us from giving. If you want to do something right, help hurting people! It helps to drain the greed from our souls. "Sow your seed." Do the task which is in front of you. Take up that opportunity to give when it comes, and invest knowing that the return will be from the hand of God when you are in need.

Two of our Lord's favorite paradoxes were, "He who loves his life loses it," and, "The measure you give will be the measure you get" (John 12:25; Matt. 7:2). The life-changing words delivered by the priest to Jean Val Jean in Victor Hugo's *Les Miserables* were, "Life is to give, not to take." Jesus said, "It is more blessed to give than to receive"

(Acts 20:35). In addition to this secret (sowing seeds) of Kohelet, the Bible reveals three additional principles in 2 Corinthians 9:

1. The principle of increase: "Now this I say, he who sows sparingly will also reap sparingly, and he who sows bountifully will also reap bountifully" (2 Cor. 9:6). Stewardship only increases when sowing increases.
2. The principle of intent: "Each one must do just as he has purposed in his heart, not grudgingly or under compulsion, for God loves a cheerful giver" (2 Cor. 9:7). My intention is not for gain, but to please and honor God.
3. The principle of investment: "And God is able to make all grace abound to you, so that always having all sufficiency in everything you may have an abundance for every good deed...Now He who supplies seed to the sower and bread for food will supply and multiply your seed for sowing and increase the harvest of your righteousness" (2 Cor. 9:8, 10). "The harvest of your righteousness" is that our investments will cause others to also praise and honor God.

I will cast my bread on the water and trust in His promise to take care of me! Be wise. Be generous.

CHAPTER 25

The Days of Our Life
Ecclesiastes 11:7-10

—ᚱᚱ—

The Shorter Catechism begins with the question, "What is the chief end of man?" The answer to the question is, "To glorify God and to enjoy him forever." How do we enjoy God? How do you enjoy anyone? We tend to enjoy the people who make us feel loved. We simply enjoy their presence.

How then has God made us feel loved? He has touched our greatest needs with His kindness. What has He told us to enjoy about Himself? Paul says it is "God who richly supplies us with all things to enjoy" (1 Tim. 6:17b). However, approximately one thousand years before Paul, Solomon issued this disclaimer. In chapter 2 he said, *"For who can eat and who can have enjoyment without him?"* (Eccl. 2:25). He has given us all things to enjoy but we cannot enjoy them without Him! The secrets of Kohelet in chapter 11 reveal how to enjoy God.

Remember to Enjoy the Days You Have, 11:7-8
"The light is pleasant, and it is good for the eyes to see the sun" (Eccl. 11:7). This is a poetic expression of enjoying

199

life while picturing the sun rising in the morning, filling the creation with hues of colors and texture, warming your face and making you thankful that you are alive. God, the Creator of it all, gives Himself and all that He has created to be enjoyed. But how is it enjoyed?

"Indeed, if a man should live many years, let him rejoice in them all, and let him remember the days of darkness, for they will be many. Everything that is to come will be futility" *(Eccl. 11:8)*. If you understand this verse, then you understand *Ecclesiastes*. A man who lives many years should "rejoice in them all." Each day, each month, each year should be cherished. But let's be honest. We all have bad days. Can we really cherish the days of betrayal, heartache, misery, poor health, and lay-offs? How can we enjoy every day when, truthfully, not all days are enjoyable? Solomon is not one to sugarcoat things. He is up front about this when he says, "And let him remember the days of darkness, for they shall be many."

Some commentators believe that this text refers to aging and the days of old age distinguished from the glowing light of youth, but he addresses that later in the next chapter. Others feel it is a reference to days of misfortune contrasted with the light of prosperity. However, the most probable interpretation is that the text is speaking of disappointment and frustration. This is how the Hebrew word *choshek* is used earlier by Solomon in 5:17.[1] Another dimension of this gloom would be those times of confusion when we don't know which side is up, like tripping over things in a dark room.[2]

However, there is another interpretation of "the days of darkness." Understanding death can actually help develop a better appreciation for life. We live both as mortals and immortals at the same time. As "mortals" we live in the natural world, "under the sun," and we need to enjoy these days in God's created natural world; however, we are simultaneously living in the supernatural world. To have everlasting life means to have a beginning but no end. We are also taught that there is yet still another creation referred to as a "new heavens and a new earth" (Rev. 21:1). As immortals, we shall enjoy that eternal kingdom. Solomon, however, is giving us counsel about how to enjoy the "nasty now and now" in light of the "sweet by and by."

The last statement of verse 8 says, "Everything that is to come will be futility." For translation purposes, this is somewhat disturbing to hear in English; but Solomon is book-ending his teaching and returns to his opening statement. Solomon's point is that this mortal life will pass quickly, and we might as well enjoy it with every breath. Ancient Egyptians carried the figure of a corpse among banquet guests. This wasn't to dampen the party but rather enhance it. They were saying, "Eat, drink and be merry! For tomorrow we die!" It gave some perspective to life. Life should be lived in the now, which moves Solomon to his next point.

Remember That the Days You Have Are Now, 11:9-10

How do we enjoy the present in spite of aging, gloom, and confusion? How do we enjoy life, knowing that we are one day closer to death? At this point, there should be no doubt in our minds that God's desire for us is to enjoy the days of our lives "under the sun." Eat, drink, enjoy your spouse, your work and enjoy your play (Eccl. 2:24; 3:12-13, 22; 5:18; 8:15; 9:7-9). In the following two verses he gives us the key. It is a key with four teeth to unlock the door to living and enjoying our days. It will also reveal how to land on both feet each day. Look at the first one…

Try letting your heart be pleasant. "Rejoice, young man, during your childhood, and let your heart be pleasant during the days of young manhood" (Eccl. 11:9a). "Rejoice"; learn how to cultivate joy while you are young. Patterns are established while we are adolescents, and they affect our entire lives. The warning is given here to the "young man" so that he can begin to set wise patterns for his life.

What does he mean, "let your heart be pleasant?" Literally, it is "make your heart good." How? Surprisingly, by "following the impulses of your heart and the desires of your eyes." You may have the same question I had about this: how does this fit with Moses' warning in Numbers 15:39-40, "Remember all the commandments of the Lord, so as to do them and not follow after your own heart and your own eyes, after which you played the harlot, in order that you may remember to do all my commandments and be holy to you God."?

The context of Moses' warning was unlawful pleasures from an evil heart. The context of Solomon's admonishment, however, is making a *good* heart. What's the difference? The difference is a godly heart. Philippians 2:13 says, "For it is God who is at work in you, both to will and to work for His good pleasure."

Remember, God brings judgment: "And follow the impulses of your heart and the desires of your eyes. Yet know that God will bring you to judgment for all these things" (Eccl. 11:9b).

This is a healthy reminder that freedom necessitates responsibility. To utilize freedom wisely requires the foresight of its consequences. That is, responsibility to reckon with the facts. Realize the accountability; being secure within those parameters provides safety and enjoyment. Children who come from homes where rules and consequences of breaking the rules were clearly established grow up with greater confidence. Knowing that God has set the boundaries to my freedom, I can rest and enjoy my freedom.

Try removing vexation from your life: "So, remove grief and anger from your heart" (Eccl. 11:10a). The word is "bitterness," which is another way of saying "resentment." The Bible says, "Let all bitterness, wrath, anger, clamor and slander be put away from you along with all malice. Be kind to one another, tender-hearted, forgiving each other, just as God in Christ also has forgiven you" (Eph. 4:31-32). In the book of Hebrews, we are told, "Pursue peace with all men, and the sanctification without which no one will see the Lord. See to it that no one comes short of the grace of God; that no root of bitterness springing up causes trouble, and by it many are defiled" (Heb. 12:14-15). All of us have experienced deep disappointment which if left unchecked becomes bitterness. Bitter roots will produce bitter fruit. Bitterness on the inside will eventually show itself, and it will destroy any chance for enjoying your days on this earth. Forgiveness is actually a means to the freedom to enjoy your days.

Try putting away pain from your body: "*And put away pain from your body, because childhood and the prime of life are fleeting*" (Eccl. 11:10b). Get rid of the things that are causing or will cause your body pain. All of us are living in temporary housing. Our souls reside in these bodies for the duration of our time "under the sun." Therefore, strive to remove those things that will break you body down whether it be bitterness and anger or addictive behaviors or addictive substances. Life is short. Do you really want to lose the freedom to enjoy your days because of what you did to yourself in your youth? We are not guaranteed a tomorrow. Would you really want to spend your last day on earth being bitter at yourself for your own foolishness? Of course you wouldn't! Rather, you would want to seize the day for all its worth. There is still much to enjoy and celebrate. These are decisions we need to be making now!

This word "childhood" is used only here in the Old Testament and means while your hair is black! Now is the time to take the counsel of a wise old man. I want to encourage you to invest in your body now. Now is the time to stop smoking and abusing alcohol or drugs. Now is the time to start eating better. Now is the time to exercise. Remember, we reside in temporary housing, and it's the only housing we have. Take good care of it.

Take the key. Unlock the secret. Life is vaporous and passes quickly. Seize it! Enjoy it, but remember to live it daily. Turn the key and open the door to enjoying the life God has given you. Enjoy the days you have, and remember that the days you have *are now*.

CHAPTER 26

Wisdom for the Aging
Ecclesiastes 12:1-8

—ɯ—

D r. Herbert Lockyer was a well known Bible lecturer
whose life and ministry continued well into his nine-
ties. He wrote: "Benjamin Desraeli must have had a chip
on his shoulder when he wrote in *Coningsby*: 'Youth is a
blunder; manhood a struggle; old age regret.' Since I have
passed my 93rd milestone on life's' pilgrimage (I was born
on September 10, 1886), I am a living lie to old age being
a regret. Certainly, as I look back over past years, I have
many regrets; but I have no distress of mind over being an
old man. I am deliciously satisfied and contented, in spite of
the fact that I am now "old and gray headed," as the Psalmist
expresses it, and am daily proving that 'Godliness with
contentment is great gain.'"

We hear the jokes about aging. You know you are old
when:

"The gleam in your eye is from the sun hitting your
bifocals."
"You get winded playing checkers."
"Your mind writes checks that your body can't cash."

"Your knees buckle, but your belt won't."
"Everything hurts, and what doesn't hurt, doesn't work."

But not everyone is laughing. Gerhard Newbeck, a professor from the University of Minnesota writes: "Getting older is to get further and further away from my beginnings. In spite of smart insights and sophisticated second guessing, the truth is that for me, getting older is a burdensome beast. Relentlessly, the aging proceeds. I can make it more bearable and make the proverbial best of it; but I cannot modify it. My existence is running out of time."[1]

A New York University survey found that 40 percent of Americans are terrified of growing old. There is even a term for it now, "gerontophobia," the fear of growing old. Much of the reason for this fear is known as "ageism." It works like racism. Martin Luther King Jr. said, "I have a dream that one day I will be judged by the content of my character and not by the color of my skin." The elderly also seek to be judged by the content of their character and not by the number of their years. Ageism utilizes years to pass judgment for a person's worth.

In *Life's Second Half*, Jerome Ellison has a chapter entitled "Our Strange Tribal Rites." One of those "rites" is the ritual of "shunning." In many primitive tribes, if a person is found guilty of a serious crime, he is ostracized from the tribe. Having lost his will to live, the ostracized will often become ill and die. Ellison goes on to say that we, too, use shunning in our culture toward the elderly. We all know this, and perhaps this is one reason why so many of us fear growing old; we somehow hope we'll be an exception to the rule.

It was quite different in the days of the Old Testament (Lev. 19:32). There was a saying among the Jews, "He who receives and takes care of an old man is rewarded as if he received and sought God." It seems getting and growing older is so relative. Some years ago, I was walking with my father by a swimming pool. His eye caught sight of a few ladies in bathing suits sunning themselves. Trying to impress me with his spiritual discernment, he remarked, "Darryl, isn't that just terrible?" I asked him, "How terrible is it, Dad?" He said, with a twinkle in his eye, "It's terrible to be seventy-four." And yet when Oliver Wendell Holmes, Jr., at the age of ninety-two saw a pretty girl, his response was, "Oh, what I would give to be seventy again." Now, in the final chapter of *Ecclesiastes*, Solomon has some things to say about getting old. He has a closing word to the aging, and since none of us are getting any younger, he has a word for all of us.

An Honest Word to the Aging, 12:1-5

Throughout Ecclesiastes, Solomon has not pulled any punches with us, but has laid out reality in total honesty. Here in these first five verses of chapter 12, Solomon tells us that aging is not fun so don't it expect it to be. I have a t-shirt that says, "Aging Isn't for Sissies!" It sits next to my "Old Guys Rule!" t-shirt.

"Remember also your Creator in the days of your youth, before the evil days come and the years draw near when you will say, 'I have no delight in them'" (Eccl. 12:1). This remembering is not just making a mental note of God's existence but rather acknowledging His presence in your daily life. If you want to enjoy your elderly years, you'll need to develop a better perspective of God's presence with you now. Youth is the time to prepare for aging. This intimate relationship needs to develop "before the evil days come." These "evil days" are the ones in which you will say "I have no delight in them." They are the days you are "old."

Why would we have "no delight" in being old? This advice reinforces the wisdom of Ecclesiastes 11:9, *"Be happy, young man, while you are young and let your heart give you joy in the days of your youth. Follow the ways of your heart and whatever your eyes see, but know that for all these things God will bring you to judgment" (NIV).*

"Before the sun and the light, the moon and the stars are darkened, and clouds return after the rain" (Eccl. 12:2). Most of the year, in that part of the world, the sun shone brightly every day. But after the autumn rains, the chill of winter could be felt. The clouds would turn the sunlight into gloom and block the light from the moon and the stars. These clouded skies were the signs of winter, similar to old age when physical pains are multiplied and the pleasures few. In earlier days, the rains came and the clouds disappeared leaving a clear sky. But now, it doesn't get better. The storms follow one after another. The sorrows and disappointments just keep coming. The picture now changes from the season of winter to a great household in decline. The picture here is a sad one, a slow but certain decay. It is a hastening to ...

"In the day that the watchmen of the house tremble, and mighty men stoop, the grinding ones stand idle because they are few, and those who look through windows grow dim; and the doors on the street are shut as the sound of the grinding mill is low, and one will arise at the sound of the bird, and all the daughters of song will sing softly. Furthermore, men are afraid of a high place and of terrors on the road; the almond tree blossoms, the grasshopper drags himself along, and the caperberry is ineffective. For man goes to his eternal home while mourners go about in the street..." (Eccl. 12:3-5).

1. *"The watchmen of the house tremble"* Evidently represents hands and arms trembling in weakness. They used to provide protection but now provide little strength at all.
2. *"The mighty men stoop"* The strength that held up the house, the legs now bent and bowed were once robust, but now are beginning to bend under the burden of the weight.

3. *"The grinding ones stand idle"* The teeth which used to chew our food are idle because they are few.
4. *"Those who look through the windows grow dim"* When the eyes go dim, enjoying the beauty of creation or small-print books is only a memory.
5. *"The doors on the street are shut"* Due to loss of hearing, the doors to conversation and social interaction begin to close.
6. *"One will arise at the sound of the bird"* Have you ever noticed that the elderly are up at the crack of dawn? One Florida vacation, my wife and I decided to get up early to watch the sunrise. I thought that we would have the whole beach to ourselves. To my utter amazement senior citizens were everywhere.
7. *"All the daughters of song will sing softly"* This phrase was utilized in ancient Ugaritc[2] literature to denote a loss of hearing. The old voices were slowly taken and now could barely speak.
8. *"Men are afraid of a high place and of terrors on the road"* Basically, you know you're old when you don't want to go to a baseball game because you don't want to drive home in the dark. In your youth, this wasn't an issue.
9. *"The almond tree blossoms"* At first the blooms of an almond tree are pinkish in color, but when they are ready to drop, the tree is covered with snow-white blossoms. The hair becomes white with age.
10. *"The grasshopper drags himself along"* Normally agile and able to leap great bounds, now its gait is slow and its movement fragile.
11. *"The caperberry is ineffective"* The "caperberry" was used to stimulate the sensual appetite. In parts of the ancient Near East, caperberries were considered an aphrodisiac. This implies a loss of sexual appetite or potency in old age. The inhabitant is on

the brink of leaving. Age is marked not only by the loss of pleasure but the imminence of death.

12. *"The mourners go about in the street."* Forthright isn't he? All of the above climaxes with death. He is describing a funeral procession.

An Honest Word of Counsel to the Aged, 12:6-8

"Remember Him before the silver cord is broken and the golden bowl is crushed, the pitcher by the well is shattered and the wheel at the cistern is crushed" (Eccl. 12:6). The imagery here captures the fragility of the human body as a precious, breakable piece of earthenware. We have now come to the final struggle, the drawing of water from a well. Here is the silver cord, the precious golden bowl, the pitcher and a wheel. If these are broken, we can no longer draw water.[3] Likewise, when the body dies, we can no longer draw breath. This is describing the moment of death.

"Then the dust will return to the earth as it was, and the spirit will return to God who gave it" (Eccl. 12:7). When the temporary housing (body) is demolished (dies), where does the inhabitant go?

Crying out with a loud voice, Jesus said, "Father, into your hands I commit my spirit. Having said this, he breathed his last" (Luke 23:46).

As he was being stoned, Stephen said, "Lord Jesus, receive my spirit" (Acts 7:59).

Death is our final enemy. And this enemy has caused most of our pain. The truth is, this decaying body is being returned to dust. Solomon is making a reference to Genesis 2:7 and 3:19. Adam was created from the dust of the earth (2:7) and, within the context of 3:19, there is the repercussion of the Fall, the returning of the body to dust. So, regarding humanity, there is a reversal of the Genesis creation account taking place here. The French poet Victor Hugo said, "For half a century I have been writing my thoughts in prose and in verse. But I feel I have not said the thousandth part of what is in me. When I go down to the grave, I can say like many others, 'I have finished my day's work.' But I cannot say, 'I have finished my life.' My day's work will begin the next morning. The tomb is not a blind alley. It is a thoroughfare. It closes on the twilight but opens on the dawn."

For obvious reasons, we tend to identify ourselves with our body. And while we can disguise age with cosmetic surgery and creams, we are still aging. Our bodies are in temporary housing. It's our souls that live forevermore.[4] When thinking of life after this body returns to dust, remember these Scriptures: Luke 23:43; John 11:25, 26; 14:1-3; 2 Cor. 5:1-8; Phil. 1:21-23; Rev. 5:9, 10; 6:9-11. We must be prepared for death. There are things we can learn now to prepare us for old age. Where do you find your value? What is your hope?

"Vanity of vanities," says the Preacher, *"all is vanity!" (Eccl. 12:8).* Solomon repeats his theme. Life is vaporous and passes quickly. Thus, at times, it appears senseless, but there is One who makes sense out of it all.

CHAPTER 27

An Understanding of Life
Ecclesiastes 12:9-14

—⚶—

*L*ife Magazine" once featured an article entitled "Why are
we here?" The article stated, "With the holiday season
upon us, 'Life' asked some wise men and women to ponder
why we are here. Scientists and Theologians, Authors and
Artists, Celebrities and everyday sages responded. The
following 'answers'...provide a medley of philosophies—
personal and, at times, profound."
Here are some excerpts from the interviews:

- Tom Robbins (writer): "Our purpose is to consciously,
  deliberately evolve toward a wiser, more liberated
  and luminous state of being; to return to Eden, make
  friends with the snake and set up our computers
  among the wild apple trees."

- Jose Martinez responded: "We're here to die, just
  live and die. I drive a cab. I do some fishing, take my
  girl out, pay taxes, do a little reading, then get ready
  to drop dead."

- Harry Blackmun (Supreme Court Justice): "Not one
  of us asked to be here or had very much to do with

his arrival. With our finite minds we cannot presume to know if there is a purpose. We sense, however, the presence of something greater than we can comprehend, a force as yet unknown to us—perhaps to be unknown."

- Raimon Panikkar (a Hindu scholar): "To look for a purpose in life outside life itself amounts to killing life. Reason is given by life, not vice versa. Life is prior to meaning. Life does not die, sing the Vedas... Human life is joyful interrogation. Any answer is blasphemy."

- Garrison Keillor (humorist): "To know and to serve God, of course, is why we're here, a clear truth that, like the nose on your face, is near at hand and easily discernible but can make you dizzy if you try to focus on it too hard.

- John Cage (composer): "No 'why'; just 'here.'"

- Mike Ditka (former coach of the Chicago Bears): "I believe we're here for a reason. I believe that I'm created by God to do the job that he's given me while I'm here, to serve him and then to return to him. But it took me a long time to understand this."

- Jackie Mason (comedian) said: "People call it truth, religion; I call it insanity, the denial of death as the basic truth of life. 'What is the meaning of life?' is a stupid question. Life just exists. You say to yourself, 'I can't accept that I mean nothing, so I have to find the meaning of life so that I won't mean as little as I know I do.'"

- Willie Nelson (country western artist): "The purpose of life is to reach perfection. The rose starts as a seed, then grows with the sunshine and the rain. After a period of time, the perfect rose blossoms. The human experience is much the same except that the time span is much greater because man, before he can reach this state of perfection, must return again and again through many incarnations to conquer all disease, greed, jealousy, anger, hatred and guilt."

- Leonard Nimoy (actor, Mr. Spock): "I find the question 'why are we here?' typically human. I'd suggest that 'are we here?' would be the more a logical choice."[1]

At Christmas we tend to reflect on those special things that make life worth living. Followed by a new year, some often ponder the meaning of existence, while others avoid the topic altogether.

If *Life* magazine had asked you, "Why are we here? What is the meaning of your existence?" What would you have said?

Almost three thousand years ago a true sage reflected on his life, and Solomon concluded his journal with his answer to that particular question: why are we here? What is the meaning of life? As we have already learned, life "under the sun" is vaporous, passing quickly. To understand what *can* be understood, it must be slowed down and examined. This is what Solomon has done for us. We need to understand what can be understood. This is how we will make the most of our lives. Solomon puts wisdom to words.

Wisdom Put into Words, 12:9-10

"In addition to being a wise man, the Preacher also taught the people knowledge; and he pondered, searched out and arranged many proverbs" (Eccl. 12:9). The "wise man" is one who has mastered the art of living. He is the "Preacher." Remember *Kohelet*, the sage who "taught the people knowledge." This knowledge is more than mere facts about life. It is the skill and the discipline that lead to freedoms, goals and priorities that issue from a creed of

life. Notice here that he had "pondered," "searched out" and "arranged" many proverbs.

As one scholar has observed, this current generation may be the first in civilized times that has not raised its young on proverbs. From the beginning of recorded history, proverbs have been a standard way of summarizing life's experiences. In our own country, both the biblical proverbs of Solomon and the Anglo-Saxon wisdom collected in *Poor Richard's Almanac* by Benjamin Franklin have helped generations understand the art of successful living.

Proverbs are short, pithy sayings of raw observable truth about life. He "pondered," weighed and evaluated what he said. He "searched out," was diligent and thorough; he "arranged" and put into order. In his book of *Proverbs*, the first nine chapters are really not proverbs at all, but a compilation of instruction.[2] This was not casual reminiscing, but intentional research of the meaning of life.

"The Preacher sought to find delightful words and to write words of truth correctly" (Eccl. 12:10). The words he used were picked carefully, "delightful words," words which would encourage. This was to be something good for us, not depressing nor damaging. Solomon's words are *yoshe*, which means "straight." These are words that are true and inerrant. Because of that, these words were placed like nails which pierce us at times.

Words Nailed to Reality, 12:11-12

"The words of wise men are like goads, and masters of these collections are like well-driven nails; they are given by one Shepherd"(Eccl. 12:11). "Goads" are sticks with pointed ends. Wise men speak sharp pointed words to motivate right thinking.

1. These words are "like well-driven nails" and could hold the weight of any pressure of raw life.

2. The words are given by "the Shepherd." Who is the Shepherd? Perhaps he was reflecting on what his father had said in Psalm 23:1, "The Lord is my shepherd."

In Psalm 80:1-3, the psalmist wrote, "Oh, give ear, Shepherd of Israel, you who lead Joseph like a flock; you who are enthroned above the cherubim, shine forth! Before Ephraim and Benjamin and Manasseh, stir up your power and come to save us! O God, restore us and cause your face to shine upon us and we will be saved." These are not the opinions of Solomon! These words are from God Himself, and this collection of words are to stimulate and establish our creed for life. Do you have a creed for life?

"But beyond this, my son, be warned: the writing of many books is endless, and excessive devotion to books is wearying to the body" (Eccl. 12:12). This is what we call a double ending. The first one was in verse 9, "in addition to..." The second is here, "But beyond this..." Its purpose is to strengthen what he is about to say. He quotes two popular proverbs of that day: "The writing of many books is endless."

"Excessive devotion to books is wearying to the body." While, cynically, this was our theme verse in seminary, the point is that in all our learning, we must not forget the ultimate purpose: It must lead you to conclusions. There is an atmosphere in academic circles to be less tolerant of answers and more impressed with questions. In *The Great Divorce*,[3] C. S. Lewis captures this very tone. In a heaven scene, a lifelong "searcher" is being invited in. He is told by the white spirit: "I can promise you...no scope for your talents; only forgiveness for having perverted them. No atmosphere of inquiry, for I will bring you to the land not of questions but of answers, and you shall see the face of God."

But the "searcher" responds: "Ah, but we must all interpret those beautiful words in our own way! For me there is no such thing as a final answer. The free wind of inquiry must always continue to blow through the mind, must it not?"

Knowledge and cynicism appear to walk hand in hand. As Chuck Swindoll has observed: "Those who land with both feet on hard-and-fast answers in life are criticized for committing intellectual suicide. It makes things appear too simplistic, we're told. It's sophisticated to speak of how complex issues really are. The brighter the student, the more he or she is supposed to frown and question rather than smile and rest easy."[4]

The purpose of teaching is to learn something. Learning is to lead you somewhere, and that somewhere is verse 13. He now gathers up the whole book into two sentences.

The Revised Version: "This is the end of the matter."
King James Version: "Let us hear the conclusion of the whole matter."
The Amplified Version: "All has been heard; the end of the matter."
The New International Version: "Now all has been heard."
The Message: "The last and final word is this"
Darryl's Version: "Here's the Deal!"

And So, What Conclusions Do We Draw? 12:13-14

"The conclusion, when all has been heard, is: fear God and keep His commandments, because this applies to every person" (Eccl. 12:13, NASB). The literal word-for-word rendering from the Hebrew manuscript would be: "God fear...His commandments keep." We are to fear *Ha elohim*, the Creator of all "Under the Sun." Fear the One who created life with all its mysteries and apparent senselessness. When you can't figure Him out, you must still fear Him. For either

you will fear the Creator or fear the Creation. It takes the greater fear to dispel a lesser fear. But what does it mean to fear God?

It begs for us to once again speak of the Ten Commandments received at Mount Sinai which brought terror to the Israelites. "Moses said to the people, "Do not be afraid; for God has come in order to test you, and in order that the fear of Him may remain with you, so that you may not sin." They were frightened by God in order that they would understand that *He is God*! God then took the terror out of the fearing and left us with a wonderful sense of honor and reverence.

"For God will bring every act to judgment, everything which is hidden, whether it is good or evil" (Eccl. 12:14). Judgment will determine how human you were. Paul says in 1 Corinthians 4:5, "Therefore do not go on passing judgment before the time, but wait until the Lord comes who will both bring to light the things hidden in the darkness and disclose the motives of men's hearts; and then each man's praise will come to him from God." We will give an account for our lives whether we like it or not.

Life is a gift given to us from the hand of God, vaporous and, thus, passing through our fingers at a great pace. But wisdom is remembering the moments and giving thanks for the goodness and trusting Him in the badness. Life is lived in response to life itself. In the end, all that is wrong will be made right, and all that is right will be rewarded. Life can be *hevel*, but it's a gift worth taking!

APPENDIX

What is the Gospel?

—ɯ—

B ecause we have made some poor choices and mistakes
(what the Bible calls sin) in life, we have missed the
standard that God has set for us. As a result of sin, we are
separated from God. There is no way that we can earn or
merit everlasting life, but the Good News is that God has
initiated peace with us. This is why (in the Christmas Story)
the Angel of the Lord told the shepherds, "I bring you good
news of great joy which shall be for all people. Today...a
Savior has been born to you; He is Christ the Lord" (Luke 2:
10-11). This Savior (Rescuer) was Jesus. Since He is God,
He alone has the credentials to offer forgiveness and everlasting life.

Imagine you have cancer cells in your body that will
eventually kill you, yet there is a medical way that your
cancer cells can be extracted from you and placed into my
body. What would happen to you? You would live. But, what
would happen to me? I would die. The truth of the matter
is that all of humanity has a sin virus, but unlike cancer it
has eternal repercussions. The Good News is that Jesus has
offered to remove these "sin cells" in order that you can have
everlasting life. This is what Christians call "born again."
The Bible says that Jesus took the penalty for our sins and

placed it on Himself when He was crucified on the Cross. "God demonstrates His own love toward us, in that while we were yet sinners, Christ died for us" (Rom. 5:8).

The Good News is that, because Jesus is God, He rose again three days later after being crucified, demonstrating His victory over sin and death. That is why to this day, Christians celebrate Easter. Therefore, if you are willing to ask Jesus to forgive your sins and to place your faith in Him alone for your salvation, rather than in works, you can be born again. The Bible says, "For by grace you have been saved through faith, and not of yourselves; it is the gift of God, not of works, that no one should boast" (Eph. 2:8, 9).

Would you like to tell God that you are sorry for your sins and turn your life over to Him? If yes, in your own words pray the following:

"Dear God, I know that I am a sinner. I am so sorry for my sins and know that I deserve death. I believe that Jesus died for my sins and rose from the grave. I trust you now for my salvation. Thank you for forgiveness and everlasting life. In Jesus name, amen."

Remember that it's not the prayer that saves you, but trusting in Jesus for your forgiveness and salvation that saves you.

Now what? Tell another Christian that you are born again. Begin to read the Bible (start with the book of John in the New Testament). Begin to spend time praying. Find other believers. Spend time with them and worship with them. Drop me an email, and I'd be glad to answer your questions on getting started (rkbrewer@hotmail.com).

ENDNOTES

—ᴍ—

Foreword
[1] *The NIV Study Bible*, Introduction to Ecclesiastes, "Literary Features", p. 1006.

Chapter 1
[1] First five books of the Bible are also known as the Law or the Pentateuch.

Chapter 2
[1] Grammatically, this is known as a superlative genitive.
[2] For example, "Lord of lords", "Holy of holies", "King of kings."
[3] The goal here is not to provide a science lesson. Rather, the author is simply utilizing an illustration to make a spiritual point relating to his listeners and readers.

Chapter 3
[1] This is referred to as a "chaism," a clue in regard to highlighting the author's main point. The "bookends" indicates that the primary point is in the middle, e.g. 1:15 would, in this case, be the primary point.
[2] Solomon is also the author of most of the proverbs contained within the book of Proverbs.

[3] Postmodernism is a term used to describe both a worldview and an era (1973 to present) of loosely connected trends, ideologies, and cultural characteristics which primarily embrace relativism, pluralism, spiritual curiosity, and a general ignorance and suspicion of Christian beliefs. To learn more, read *Postmodernism: What You Should Know and do About It* (2nd edition) by Robert Brewer (New York: Writer's Showcase, 2002).

[4] Jim Powell, *Postmodernism for Beginners* (New York: Writers & Readers Inc., 1998), p. 10.

[5] Paul Feyeraberd, *Farewell to Reason* (New York: Verso, 1987), back cover.

[6] In Eccl. 1:16, Solomon is not grammatically limiting himself to the kings of Israel (i.e. Saul and David); possibly including Canaanite kings who preceded him. Regardless, we know from 1 Kings 10:23 that Solomon was greater than all of the kings of the earth.

[7] Dr. Ron Allen, a Dallas Seminary professor, once shared with me an encounter he had with a Roman Catholic who practiced the monastic vow of silence. The student asked Dr. Allen, "How many hours of a day do you take for thought?"

Chapter 4

[1] Interestingly, the word for "parks" is derived from the word "Pardesim" from the Greek word "Paradeisos" and where we get the word "paradise."

[2] "Solomon's provision for one day was thirty kors of fine flour and sixty kors of meal, ten fat oxen, twenty pasture-fed oxen, a hundred sheep, besides dear, gazelles, roebucks, and fattened fowl" (1 Kings 4:22-23).

[3] *The Works of Josephus*, "The Antiquities of the Jews," Book 8, chapter 7:3.

[4] It appears that this was the catalyst that led to Solomon's moral demise. Nehemiah 13:26 says, "Did not Solomon, king of Israel sin regarding these things? Yet, among the many

nations, there was no king like him, and he was loved by his God, and God made him king over all of Israel; nevertheless, the foreign women caused him to sin." The lesson here being that even someone as wise as Solomon was unable to survive the influence of wives who were of different faiths.

Chapter 5

[1] "In His Own Words," *People Magazine* (November 28, 1983), Vol. 20, No. 22, p. 99.
[2] Syllogism: A formal deductive argument composed of a major premise, a minor premise, and a conclusion.
[3] Jim Collins, *Good to Great* (New York: HarperBusiness, 2001), p. 210.

Chapter 6

[1] Furthermore, we know that "man is made in the image of God" (Gen 1:27) and, thus, to kill another human is to attack the very image of God in him.
[2] There is a biblical mandate behind the life-for-life mandate (capital punishment) based on the Noahic covenant in Genesis 9, in the Mosaic law, and in the New Testament. It teaches that deliberately killing a human being created in the image of God can qualify one for capital punishment. (Christ objected to the misuse of this civil code for personal and private vengeance. See Matt. 5:38-39 within the context of Ex. 21:23-24). However, the ethical directives of a life-for-life policy in the Old Testament for premeditated murders is validated in the New Testament by statements from the Apostle Paul with regard to the civil authorities (Rom. 13:4). This is authority derived from God and under obligation to extend protection to society at large from violent criminals which sometimes results in capital punishment. Biblically, if government is performing its proper function for society, it will restrain by force those who are a violent and criminal threat to society. The implication of the Romans 13 text is that by failing to

apply the sword as punishment, the authorities "praise" evil and negate what is good. The death penalty is not an initiation of force as in murder, rather, it is a response to violent force. Whereas private vengeance is prohibited in Romans 12, permission for the government to administer action in the form of a "death penalty" for murder follows in the immediate context ("Capital Punishment," *Ask Pastor Darryl: 121 Answers to the Most Frequently Asked Bible Questions*, by Darryl DelHousaye and Bobby Brewer, SBC Press, 2002).

Chapter 8
[1] C.F. Keil, F, Delitzsch, *Keil & Delitzsch Commentary on the Old Testament: Proverbs, Ecclesiastes, Song of Solomon* (Hendrickson Publishers, 1966).
[2] Seen in the movie, *The Aviator*, Warner Bros, 2004.
[3] Leslie Brandt, *Psalms Now* (Concordia Publishing House, January 2004).

Chapter 9
[1] Tim Hansel, *You Gotta Keep Dancin'* (David C. Cook, 1985).

Chapter 10
[1] Author's note: Notice the utilization of the words "rarely" and "most" in this sentence. God does, on occasion, speak to His people through dreams (e.g. Daniel and Joseph).
[2] Matt Redman, *The Heart of Worship Files*, 2003, p. 14.

Chapter 11
[1] Interestingly, in Argentina, it is more appropriate to say, "I am satisfied" rather than "I am full" to communicate that you have finished eating.
[2] Hoarding wealth: Solomon will address this in Chapter 11.
[3] See http://www.snopes.com/glurge/fortune.asp?print=y for Glurge titled "Fortunate Sons."

Chapter 13
[1] The Hebrew word used here is *nahat*, and it implies a state of satisfaction—to be pleased.

Chapter 14
[1] Synapse: the place at which a nervous impulse passes from one neuron to another. (*Merriam-Webster's Medical Desk Dictionary, Revised Edition*, 2002).

Chapter 15
[1] Oswald Chambers, *My Utmost for His Highest* (Grand Rapids: Discovery House Publishers, 1991).
[2] Tim Hansel, *Holy Sweat* (TX: Word Books, 1987), p. 94.

Chapter 18
[1] Read Richard Wurmbrand's story in *Tortured for Christ*, (Diane Brooks, Glendale, 1969).
[2] There is some debate regarding the appropriate translation of this verse. The translators of the KJV, for example, translated this verse to say, "To his *own* hurt" (emphasis mine). However, while debatable, within the total context, it seems most likely that Solomon is referring to how authority is abused in the hands of an oppressor.
[3] Francis Schaeffer, *Christian Manifesto* (Westchester: Crossways Books, 1981), pp. 103-104.

Chapter 19
[1] This is reported to be one of the reasons that people are lured into Satanism.

Chapter 20
[1] Michael Green, *Man Alive* (InterVarsity Press, Leicester, 1967).
[2] Walt Kaiser, *A Biblical Approach to Personal Suffering* (Chicago: Moody Press, 1982), pp. 121-130.

[3] Dogs were often used as an illustration of self-abasement or insult. For example, see 1 Sam. 17:43; 2 Sam. 9:8, 16:9.
[4] These verses seem to reference a common theme (proverb) in ancient wisdom literature.

Chapter 21
[1] e.g. Masada's siege by the Romans.

Chapter 22
[1] Regarding leaders within the church, we are instructed not to lay our hands on anyone too quickly (1 Tim. 3:6).
[2] In addition to non-biblical literature of the period, this concept is also taught in Ps. 7:17 and Prov. 26:27.

Chapter 23
[1] The most ancient biblical texts did not contain chapters and verses. As a result of Solomon's wittiness, there has always been some debate among scholars about whether verse 11 belongs in the previous section (1-10) or with the current section (12-20). More recent scholarship suggests that verse 11 is actually a chiasm, i.e., it is the main point of the section and, thus, technically, neither section can claim exclusive rights to it.
[2] Michael Eaton, *Ecclesiastes: An Introduction and Commentary* (Downer's Grove, IL: InterVarsity Press, 1983), p. 137.

Chapter 24
[1] C.S. Lewis, *Mere Christianity* (New Yoark: Harper Collins, 2001), p. 86.
[2] Midrash: Commentative and interpretative writings that hold a place in the Jewish religious tradition second only to the Bible (Old Testament).

Chapter 25

[1] It is also used in this manner in another wisdom book—Job 3:1-5. Also see Job 10:18-22; 15:20-23; Ps. 107-10-14.

[2] This, for example, is how the word is used earlier in 2:12-14, when he references days of perplexity and confusion.

Chapter 26

[1] Gerhard Neubeck, "Getting Older in My Family: A Personal Reflection", *The Family Coordinator*, Vol. 27, No. 4, pp. 445-447.

[2] The Ugaritic language is only known in the form of writings found in the lost city of Ugarit in Syria since its discovery by French archaeologists in 1928. It has been extremely important for scholars of the Old Testament in clarifying Hebrew texts and has revealed more of how Judaism used common phrases, literary idioms, and expressions employed by surrounding gentile cultures.

[3] The symbolism of water represents breath. Like water from a well, when we no longer draw breath, life is gone.

[4] To learn how you can have forgiveness and everlasting life, please see the Appendix, "What is the Gospel?"

Chapter 27

[1] "Why are we here? The Meaning of life," *Life*, December 1, 1988, pp. 76-93.

[2] Technically, the proverbs of Proverbs begin in 10:1-22:16. These 375 proverbs equal the numerical number of Solomon's name (a little artistic humor).

[3] Clive Staples Lewis, *The Great Divorce*, (The MacMillan Company, 1946).

[4] Charles Swindoll, *Living on the Ragged Edge* (Thomas Nelson, 2004), p. 361.

ABOUT THE AUTHORS

Dr. Darryl DelHousaye (D.Min., Western Seminary; M.Div., Talbot School of Theology) is the President of Phoenix Seminary. Prior to this, he served as the Senior Pastor of Scottsdale Bible Church in Arizona for twenty-five years. Darryl has a gift for presenting the Word of God with joy and a genuine love for God's truth. He is able to combine biblical truth with an engaging sense of humor to various age groups, enabling him to communicate effectively with all generations. He is also the co-author of *Servant Leadership: The Seven Distinctive Characteristics of a Servant Leader*, *Ask Pastor Darryl: 121 Answers to Frequently Asked Bible Questions*, the author of *Today for Eternity*, and the notes to the book of Acts in *The Nelson Study Bible*. Darryl resides with his wife, Holly, in Scottsdale, AZ.

Dr. Bobby Brewer (D.Min., Phoenix Seminary; M.Div., Liberty Baptist Theological Seminary) has served at Baptist, Mega, Seeker, and Emergent churches. He is a Teaching Pastor at City of Grace (a multi-site church in Scottsdale and Mesa, AZ) where he also oversees Veritgo, a ministry for College Students and Young Adults. He is the author of *Postmodernism: What You Should Know & Do About It*, *UFO's: 7 Things You Should Know*, and has co-authored two other books with Dr. DelHousaye. A first-born of Generation-X, Bobby has known Dr. DelHousaye since 1996 as a friend and mentor. Bobby drives a 1983 El Camino and lives with his wife, Kristen, in Fountain Hills, AZ.

Printed in the United States
220612BV00002B/4/P

9 781606 471142